dtv

Auf dringendes Ersuchen des Premierministers begeben sich
Sherlock Holmes und Watson auf die Spuren eines Verbre-
chers, der einen Anschlag mit verheerenden Folgen für Wirt-
schaft und Regierung androht. Ihre Suche führt sie durch das
historische London, vorbei an Buckingham Palace und Westminster Abbey, Trafalgar Square und St Paul's Cathedral bis
hin zur kürzlich eröffneten Tower Bridge. Dabei treffen sie
auf die Geister berühmter Persönlichkeiten wie etwa Prinz
Albert, Maria Stuart oder William Shakespeare, die aus ihrem
Leben erzählen und nützliche Hinweise geben. Das Buch lädt
zu einer Stadterkundung der besonderen Art ein.

John Sykes, geboren in Nordengland, studierte Geschichte
in Oxford. Bevor er nach Köln übersiedelte, lebte er in
London. Er arbeitet als Übersetzer und Stadtführer und ist
Autor zahlreicher Reiseführer.

Birgit Weber studierte Kunst und Kunstpädagogik, lebt in
Köln und arbeitet freiberuflich illustratorisch und fotografisch
an Buchprojekten mit.

John Sykes

Exploring London
with Sherlock Holmes

Mit Sherlock Holmes
durch London

dtv

Von John Sykes ist bei dtv außerdem lieferbar:
What Are The English Like. Wie ticken
die Engländer (09542)

Ausführliche Informationen über
unsere Autoren und Bücher
www.dtv.de

2019 dtv Verlagsgesellschaft mbH & Co. KG, München
Lizenzausgabe mit Genehmigung von
© 2011 traveldiary, ein Imprint der 360° medien
Übersetzung S. 39: Adolf Seubert in Lord Byrons Sämtliche Werke,
Bd. 3, Leipzig: Reclam, 1874
Zitat S. 74: Reproduced with permission of Curtis Brown, London
on behalf of The Estate of Winston S. Churchill
© The Estate of Winston S. Churchill
Zitat S. 118: © The Society of Authors, on behalf
of the Bernard Shaw Estate
Umschlaggestaltung: www.buerosued.de
Satz: Greiner & Reichel, Köln
Druck und Bindung: Druckerei C.H.Beck, Nördlingen
Gedruckt auf säurefreiem, chlorfrei gebleichtem Papier
Printed in Germany · ISBN 978-3-423-09547-1

1.

Sherlock Holmes' New Case
(221B Baker Street)

Ein neuer Fall für Sherlock Holmes
(221B Baker Street)

When you have excluded the impossible,
whatever remains, however improbable,
must be the truth.

Sherlock Holmes

In the sitting room on the first floor of 221B Baker Street, Sherlock Holmes and Dr Watson are sitting in armchairs on either side of the fireplace. No fire is burning in the grate, as the weather is warm on this day, June 30th, 1895. Watson is immersed in The Times; Holmes is filling his pipe while he leafs through a book about poisonous plants. Although mild air is wafting in through the open window, the room smells of toast and kippers, as Mrs Hudson has not yet cleared the breakfast table. From the street can be heard the cries of carriage drivers, the clip-clop of horses' hooves and the twittering of birds. Suddenly there is a loud knocking on the front door below. Holmes rises quickly from his armchair and looks out of the window.

Holmes: Watson, we have two visitors – and unless my eyes deceive me, they have arrived here separately. One of them is already known to me, but I believe the other has come with a matter of greater importance. Yes, it must be something urgent, judging by the rapid footsteps on the stairs. Come in!

Mrs Hudson opens the door. A young man is standing behind her. He is wearing dark blue breeches, a jacket of the same colour that is buttoned to the collar and adorned with gold braid, and white gloves.

Schließt man das Unmögliche aus, bleibt –
wie unwahrscheinlich auch immer sie einem
vorkommen mag – die Wahrheit.

Sherlock Holmes

Im Salon in der ersten Etage von 221B Baker Street sitzen
Sherlock Holmes und Dr. Watson in Sesseln zu beiden Seiten
des Kamins. Da es warm ist an diesem Tag, dem 30. Juni
1895, brennt kein Feuer. Watson ist in ‹The Times› vertieft.
Holmes stopft seine Pfeife und blättert dabei in einem Buch
über Giftpflanzen. Obwohl laue Luft durch den hochgezoge-
nen Fensterflügel hereinweht, riecht es nach Toast und ge-
räuchertem Bückling, denn Mrs Hudson hat den Frühstücks-
tisch noch nicht abgeräumt. Von der Straße dringen die Rufe
der Kutscher, das Geklapper von Pferdehufen und Vogel-
gezwitscher ins Zimmer. Plötzlich klopft es unten an der
Haustür. Holmes erhebt sich rasch und blickt kurz aus dem
Fenster.

Holmes: Watson, zwei Herren wollen uns besuchen – unab-
hängig voneinander, wenn ich mich nicht täusche. Einen
der Herren kenne ich, aber die Angelegenheit des anderen dürfte bedeutender sein. Ja, es ist sicher etwas
Eiliges, den Schritten auf der Treppe nach zu urteilen.
Herein!

Mrs Hudson öffnet die Tür. Hinter ihr steht ein junger Mann.
Er trägt eine dunkelblaue Hose, eine bis zum Kragen zuge-
knöpfte, mit Goldborte verzierte Jacke in derselben Farbe
und weiße Handschuhe.

Holmes: Mrs Hudson, kindly ask Mr Mays to wait below for a few minutes, but we will let our first visitor enter straight away. It's not every day that the prime minister sends us a messenger.

Messenger *(addresses Holmes, but gives Watson a sideways glance)*: Are you Mr Sherlock Holmes? Indeed I have come with a message from Lord Salisbury, but no-one except you personally may know who sent me and why.

Holmes: You can rely absolutely on Dr Watson's discretion. If the prime minister thinks it important for his business to remain confidential, then I recommend sending an official government messenger incognito, and not a member of his private household. Your livery and the carriage bearing his lordship's coat of arms are an open book to the acute observer.

Messenger *(nods)*: Of course, sir. Lord Salisbury spent the night at his London residence and received with this morning's early delivery a letter that he wishes to show you. He asks if you would do him the honour of attending him at one o'clock today in Downing Street. He asks me to inform you that the matter involves a serious threat to the kingdom.

Holmes: Please tell his lordship that I shall never hesitate to put my services at the disposal of queen and country, and shall come to Downing Street at the time requested.

The messenger takes his leave, and Mrs Hudson leads a stooping grey-haired man into the room. This visitor holds a black cap in his hands and looks at the carpet rather than meeting the gaze of Holmes and Watson.

Holmes: Mrs Hudson, bitten Sie Mr Mays, einige Minuten unten zu warten, aber lassen Sie diesen Herrn sofort eintreten. Es kommt nicht jeden Tag vor, dass der Premierminister uns einen Boten schickt.

Bote *(spricht Holmes an, wirft aber einen Seitenblick auf Watson)*: Sie sind Mr Sherlock Holmes? In der Tat überbringe ich eine Nachricht von Lord Salisbury, aber niemand außer Ihnen sollte erfahren, von wem ich komme und weshalb.

Holmes: Auf die Diskretion von Dr. Watson können Sie sich absolut verlassen. Wenn der Premierminister auf Vertraulichkeit Wert legt, dann empfehle ich, einen anonymen Regierungsboten zu schicken und nicht ein Mitglied seines privaten Haushalts. Einer aufmerksamen Person verraten Ihre Livree und die Kutsche mit dem Familienwappen einiges.

Bote *(nickt)*: Sehr wohl, Sir. Lord Salisbury übernachtete in seiner Londoner Residenz und erhielt mit der morgendlichen Post ein Schreiben, das er Ihnen zeigen möchte. Er fragt, ob Sie ihm heute um 13 Uhr in der Downing Street die Ehre erweisen würden. Ich soll Ihnen mitteilen, dass es sich um eine ernste Bedrohung für das Königreich handelt.

Holmes: Richten Sie seiner Lordschaft aus, dass ich meine Fähigkeiten selbstverständlich immer in den Dienst des Landes stelle und pünktlich in der Downing Street erscheinen werde.

Der Bote verabschiedet sich, und Mrs Hudson führt einen gebückten grauhaarigen Mann ins Zimmer. Der Besucher hält seine schwarze Mütze in den Händen, weicht den Blicken von Holmes und Watson aus und schaut zu Boden.

Holmes: Good morning, Mays! I recognised the number of your hansom cab. You were a great help to me several years ago, when I was tracking down Professor Moriarty and his accomplices. Now speak out please without fear or embarrassment: what cares are depriving you of your sleep? I see you are trying to suppress a yawn, and it's obvious that you are worried about something. This must be the first time that you come knocking at my door without whistling a merry tune.

Mays: Mr Holmes, sir, I don't want to disturb you, but something strange happened yesterday. A man hired my cab at Victoria Station and wanted to go to Buckingham Palace. I didn't like the look of this passenger – he had a grim expression, and barked commands at me. But a man can't pick and choose his customers, so I drove him to the palace. He got out there and told me to wait. After that he wanted me to drive him right across London, but we stopped again and again, and he kept disappearing for a while. I thought this was odd, and started to keep an eye on him. When he went into a pub on Fleet Street and came back again half an hour later, I noticed something: he had a false beard. I took a really good look at him – perhaps I stared too closely, because he seemed to notice it, looked right back with his nasty piercing eyes and paid me off quickly with a guinea as a tip. Now a guinea is far too much, even though I drove him around for several hours. I was thinking about this all night, tossing and turning, until at four o'clock Mrs Mays had had enough and got the whole story out of me. She said I should come and tell you, Mr Holmes.

Holmes: And quite right, too! Now please describe ex-

Holmes: Mays, guten Tag! Ich habe an der Nummer Ihrer Droschke erkannt, dass Sie es sind. Als ich vor einigen Jahren Professor Moriarty und seinen Komplizen auf der Spur war, haben Sie mir sehr geholfen. Sagen Sie uns jetzt freimütig: Welche Sorge bringt Sie um den Schlaf? Sie versuchen, ein Gähnen zu unterdrücken, und der Kummer steht Ihnen ins Gesicht geschrieben. Es ist heute sicherlich das erste Mal, dass Sie an meiner Haustür klopfen, ohne dabei ein fröhliches Lied zu pfeifen.

Mays: Mr Holmes, Sir, ich hoffe, ich störe Sie nicht, aber gestern ist etwas Merkwürdiges passiert. Am Bahnhof Victoria stieg bei mir ein Fahrgast ein und wollte zum Buckingham Palace. Der Mann gefiel mir gar nicht – er sah finster aus und gab Befehle in einem barschen Ton. Aber man kann sich seine Kundschaft nicht aussuchen. Also fuhr ich ihn zum Palast, wo er ausstieg und mich warten ließ. Dann wollte er durch die halbe Stadt, aber wir hielten immer wieder an, und er blieb eine Weile fort. Ich fand das verdächtig und behielt ihn im Auge, so gut es ging. Als er in der Fleet Street in einer Kneipe verschwand und eine halbe Stunde später wieder einstieg, fiel mir auf, dass er einen falschen Bart trug. Ich habe genau hingeschaut – vielleicht zu genau. Er hat es gemerkt, warf mir einen bösen Blick zu und entließ mich ganz schnell mit einer Guinee Trinkgeld. Das ist viel zu viel, auch wenn ich einige Stunden mit ihm unterwegs war. Vor lauter Grübeln konnte ich überhaupt nicht schlafen und wälzte mich so lange im Bett hin und her, bis Mrs Mays um vier Uhr früh genug hatte und fragte, was los sei. Sie meinte, ich sollte es Ihnen erzählen, Mr Holmes.

Holmes: Das ist ganz richtig so. Jetzt beschreiben Sie die gest-

actly the route you took. Where did he ask you to stop?
And where did this man with the false beard go after
he dismissed you?

Mays: From the palace we went to Westminster Abbey.
Then he got out again at the Houses of Parliament
and was away for a while. After that he wanted to go
along Whitehall. He took a close look at the Banqueting House, and then we were off to Trafalgar Square.
He walked round Nelson's Column three times and
cast his eye over the square from all sides. Next I drove
him down The Strand. A quick detour to Covent Garden, where he talked to a girl who sells flowers by the
church. Then the Savoy Hotel, and on towards Fleet
Street. He went through the gate to Middle Temple
Lane and disappeared for quite a long time. The last
stop was a pub: Ye Olde Cheshire Cheese, but I don't
know what for – there was no ale on his breath when he
paid me off. It all seemed so suspicious that I followed
him at a distance, all the way up the hill to St Paul's
Cathedral. He went in by a side door – but an evil-look-
ing scoundrel like that doesn't go there to worship the
Lord, I'll wager! By that time it was late, getting dark,
and I went home.

Holmes: And what, in your opinion, was this man up to?
Can you describe his appearance more precisely?

Mays: He was tall and gaunt, with a hooked nose and
staring eyes. He had straight black hair and dressed
like a gentleman – but he didn't speak like one. More
like an East End voice, but trying to sound posh. He
had a thin moustache that didn't look at all like his
bushy beard. That was what made me suspicious. I'm

rige Strecke bitte ganz genau. Wo haben Sie überall angehalten? Und wohin ging der bärtige Mann, nachdem er Sie entließ?

Mays: Vom Palast fuhren wir zur Westminster Abbey. Anschließend stieg er wieder an den Houses of Parliament aus und war lange weg. Dann wollte er entlang Whitehall fahren. Er schaute sich das Banqueting House genau an. Die nächste Station war der Trafalgar Square, wo er dreimal um die Nelson-Säule herumging und den Platz von allen Seiten in Augenschein nahm. Danach kutschierte ich ihn The Strand hinunter. Ein kurzer Abstecher zum Markt in Covent Garden, wo er mit einer Blumenverkäuferin an der Kirche sprach. Von dort zum Savoy Hotel und weiter Richtung Fleet Street. Er ging durch das Tor zur Inner Temple Lane und verschwand für einige Zeit. Die letzte Station war die Kneipe Ye Olde Cheshire Cheese. Warum, kann ich nicht sagen: Sein Atem roch nicht nach Bier, als er wieder herauskam und mich bezahlte. Es kam mir alles so suspekt vor, dass ich ihm mit etwas Abstand bis zu St Paul's Cathedral folgte. Dort trat er durch eine Seitentür hinein – aber so ein verdorben aussehender Schurke geht bestimmt nicht zum Gottesdienst! Da es schon spät war und dunkel wurde, fuhr ich nach Hause.

Holmes: Was hatte dieser Mann Ihrer Meinung nach vor? Können Sie seine Person etwas näher beschreiben?

Mays: Er war groß und hager, hatte eine Hakennase und stierende Augen. Glatte schwarze Haare, angezogen wie ein Gentleman – aber so gesprochen hat er nicht. Er klang wie einer aus dem East End, der vornehm klingen will. Er hatte einen dünnen Oberlippenbart, der gar nicht zum buschigen Kinnbart passte. Das war es, was mich stutzig machte.

sure he was scouting something out yesterday, Mr
Holmes. Sometimes he told me to stop, then just sat
in the cab and watched – in places where he didn't
want to be seen, I suppose. And then at other places
he got out and started sniffing around after something.

Holmes: Mays, I am most grateful to you. Take this for
your trouble, and please let me know if you see or
hear anything more of this man.

The cab driver accepts a coin and leaves. Holmes walks
to and fro across the room. Watson knows his friend
too well to interrupt the great detective's thoughts immediately, but after a few minutes he can no longer
contain himself.

Watson: Two mysterious new cases at the same time,
Holmes! And in four hours you have an appointment
with the prime minister. I suppose you will want to
pay a visit to the barber, so that you look your best in
Downing Street?

Holmes: Certainly not! We can't waste time on vanity.
I hope you have no pressing business, Watson, as I
shall need your assistance all day. And don't imagine
for a moment that what we have just heard amounts
to two separate cases. We must leave for the palace
without delay!

Holmes' famous address, 221B Baker Street, does not
exist, but many buildings in Baker Street are a good
match for the detective's home as it is described in
the stories by Sir Arthur Conan Doyle. One of them,
situated between numbers 237 and 239, is now

Mr Holmes, ich bin mir sicher, dass er gestern etwas ausgekundschaftet hat. Manchmal befahl er mir anzuhalten, blieb dann in der Droschke sitzen und sah sich um – wahrscheinlich Orte, an denen er nicht auffallen wollte. Und andernorts stieg er aus und schnüffelte herum.

Holmes: Vielen Dank für Ihren Besuch, Mays. Nehmen Sie das hier für Ihre Mühen, und lassen Sie mich bitte wissen, wenn Sie diesen Mann sehen oder etwas von ihm hören.

Der Droschkenfahrer nimmt eine Münze entgegen und geht. Holmes schreitet im Zimmer auf und ab. Watson kennt seinen Freund nur zu gut und weiß, dass er die Gedanken des großen Detektivs nicht unterbrechen sollte, doch nach einigen Minuten kann er sich nicht mehr zurückhalten.

Watson: Zwei seltsame neue Fälle auf einmal, Holmes! Und bereits in vier Stunden haben Sie eine Audienz beim Premierminister. Wollen Sie vielleicht vorher zum Barbier gehen, damit Sie sich in Downing Street von Ihrer besten Seite zeigen können?

Holmes: Keinesfalls! Wir dürfen keine Zeit für Eitelkeiten verschwenden. Ich hoffe, Sie haben heute nichts Wichtiges vor, Watson, denn ich werde Ihre Unterstützung den ganzen Tag brauchen. Glauben Sie nicht auch nur für eine Sekunde, dass es sich hier um zwei unterschiedliche Fälle handelt. Wir müssen sofort zum Palast!

Baker Street 221B, die berühmte Adresse von Holmes, existiert nicht, aber viele Häuser in dieser Straße passen auf die Beschreibungen in den Detektivgeschichten von Sir Arthur Conan Doyle. Eines der Häuser, zwischen den Hausnummern 237 und 239,

home to the Sherlock Holmes Museum (daily 9.30 am – 6 pm, www.sherlock-holmes.co.uk), which reconstructs Holmes' apartment with praiseworthy attention to detail. A narrow staircase leads to the first floor and a sitting room like the one in which Holmes and Watson received visitors and spent much of their time. Holmes' magnifying glass, his crooked pipe and deerstalker hat can be seen on a small table. In the corner behind his armchair are glass phials and apparatus for his chemical experiments – as well as his violin, of course. Holes in the wallpaper opposite the fireplace were made by shots from Holmes' revolver. They form, with outstandingly accurate marksmanship, the letters VR: Victoria Regina, in honour of Queen Victoria.

Nearby, Sherlock Holmes can be seen at Madame Tussauds waxworks, and a bronze statue of him stands in front of Baker Street Tube station. To accompany Holmes and Watson to Buckingham Palace, either call a cab from their front door or take the Tube (Jubilee Line) from Baker Street, get off after two stops at Green Park and walk five minutes through the park to the palace. The remainder of the journey that the cab driver Mays and his mysterious passenger took from Buckingham Palace to St Paul's Cathedral can be walked in a single day, but for a more relaxed exploration of London, divide the route into two parts, with Trafalgar Square as the half-way point.

beherbergt heute das Sherlock Holmes Museum (tägliche Öffnungszeiten von 9:30-16 Uhr, www.sherlock-holmes.co.uk), eine bemerkenswert detailreiche Nachempfindung von Holmes' Zimmern. Eine enge Treppe führt in die erste Etage und in den Salon, wo Holmes und Watson sich oft aufhielten und Besucher empfingen. Auf einem kleinen Tisch liegen Holmes' Lupe, seine krumme Pfeife und seine Mütze ... In der Ecke hinter seinem Sessel stehen Fläschchen und Geräte für chemische Experimente – und natürlich seine Violine. Einschusslöcher in der Tapete gegenüber dem Kamin stammen aus Holmes' Revolver und bilden die Buchstaben VR: Victoria Regina, eine mit bemerkenswerter Zielgenauigkeit in die Wand geschossene Ehrung für die Königin Victoria.

Im nahe gelegenen Madame Tussauds kann man Sherlock Holmes als Wachsfigur sehen, vor der U-Bahn-Station Baker Street steht er als eine Bronzestatue.

Wer Holmes und Watson zum Buckingham Palace begleiten möchte, ruft entweder ein Taxi direkt vor ihre Haustür oder nimmt die U-Bahn (Jubilee Line) an der Baker Street, steigt nach zwei Stationen bei Green Park aus und geht fünf Minuten durch den Park zum Palast. Die weitere Route des Kutschers Mays und seines geheimnisvollen Fahrgasts zwischen Buckingham Palace und St Paul's Cathedral lässt sich an einem Tag zu Fuß zurücklegen. Aber für eine entspanntere Erkundung von London empfiehlt es sich, den Weg in zwei Abschnitte, mit Trafalgar Square als Mittelpunkt, aufzuteilen ...

2.

A Meeting with the Prince Consort
(Buckingham Palace)

Eine Einführung mit dem Prinzgemahl
(Buckingham Palace)

What a wonderful city to pillage!

Blücher, Prussian field marshal,
to the Duke of Wellington

The London residence of British kings and queens has its origins in a house that was built for the Duke of Buckingham in 1702 and bought 60 years later by King George III. The well-known façade of Buckingham Palace is the east side, which faces The Mall and St James's Park. On festive occasions such as royal weddings, the royal family wave to crowds of onlookers from the balcony. This balcony already existed in Sherlock Holmes' day, although the east façade of the palace, which was altered in 1912, looked different at that time. The rooms in this wing date from the reign of Queen Victoria (1837–1901). The monument in front of the palace, which was erected in her honour, is a bombastic celebration of the British Empire and its naval and commercial power. It is built of 2300 tons of white marble and crowned by the gilded figure of Victory. The palace contains 775 rooms, including 52 bedrooms for the royal family and their guests, 188 rooms for the staff, 78 bathrooms and the 19 magnificent state rooms, which are opened to the public in August and September (information: www.royalcollection.org.uk) while the Queen takes her annual holiday at Balmoral Castle. Visitors can admire paintings, sculptures, porcelain and fine English and French furniture. All year round it is possible to enter the Royal Mews to see the stables and vehicles that are used on official occasions, including a fleet of Rolls-Royces and carriages such as the Gold State Coach.

Was für eine wunderbare Stadt zum Plündern!

von Blücher, preußischer Generalfeldmarschall,
zum Herzog von Wellington

Die Londoner Residenz der britischen Monarchen geht zurück auf einen Wohnsitz, der 1702 für den Herzog von Buckingham gebaut und sechzig Jahre später von König George III. gekauft wurde. Die berühmte Fassade des Buckingham Palace ist die Ostseite mit Blick auf den Prachtboulevard The Mall und auf St James's Park. Bei feierlichen Anlässen wie königlichen Hochzeiten winken die «Royals» vom Balkon, der bereits zu Sherlock Holmes' Zeit existierte, obwohl die Ostfassade damals anders aussah, sie wurde 1912 erneuert. Die Räume in diesem Flügel stammen aus der Regierungszeit von Königin Victoria (1837-1901). Ihr zu Ehren wurde das von einer vergoldeten Siegesgöttin gekrönte Denkmal vor dem Palast errichtet, eine pompöse Huldigung des Empires und seiner Seemacht aus 2300 Tonnen weißem Marmor. Im Buckingham Palace befinden sich 775 Zimmer, darunter 52 Schlafzimmer für die königliche Familie und Gäste, 188 Zimmer für Bedienstete, 78 Badezimmer und 19 Prunksäle, die «State Rooms», die im August und September, während des jährlichen Aufenthalts der Königin im schottischen Balmoral Castle, für Besucher geöffnet sind (Auskunft: www.royalcollection.org.uk). Man kann Gemälde, Skulpturen, Porzellan und erlesene englische und französische Möbel bewundern. Ganzjährig sind in der Royal Mews die Stallungen und Staatskarossen – die goldene Kutsche, Rolls-Royce usw. – und

The neighbouring Queen's Gallery presents changing exhibitions of art from the extensive and exquisite Royal Collection.

Holmes and Watson alight from their cab not in front of the palace, but at its south side on Buckingham Gate, at the entrance to the Royal Mews.

Holmes: Palace servants and suppliers go in and out here all the time. A villain seeking entry to the palace is most likely to try his luck from here.

Watson: Who is that over there with the balding head? His clothes are so old-fashioned, his moustache and long sideburns too. He seems somehow familiar.

Holmes: Good Lord, Watson! That is the Prince Consort Albert, who died more than 30 years ago, God rest his soul. He obviously wants to tell us something.

Prince Albert: Good morning, gentlemen! I know who you are and why you have come. We ghosts have powers that mortals lack. Yes, I am Albert of Saxe-Coburg and Gotha. Even after my life has come to an end, I continue to look after my good wife Victoria. Come along, I'll show you our palace. You would like to know whether criminals could cause harm here. We'll enter through this door on the right.

He points to an entrance between two stone columns, unlocks the door and leads Holmes and Watson through a number of rooms and past the stables to the garden, where he follows a path between lawns to the rear side

nebenan in der Queen's Gallery Wechselausstellungen aus der kostbaren und umfangreichen königlichen Sammlung zu sehen.

Holmes und Watson steigen nicht vor dem Palast aus ihrer Droschke aus, sondern in der Straße Buckingham Gate an der Südseite und gehen zum Tor der Royal Mews.

Holmes: Hier gehen Bedienstete und Lieferanten ein und aus. Ein Übeltäter, der sich Zugang zum Palast verschaffen will, würde es am ehesten von dieser Seite versuchen.

Watson: Wer ist der Mann da drüben mit der Glatze? Seine Kleidung ist so altmodisch, der Oberlippenbart und die langen Koteletten ebenso. Er kommt mir irgendwie bekannt vor.

Holmes: Um Himmels willen, Watson! Das ist der Prinzgemahl Albert, der schon vor über 30 Jahren verstorben ist, Gott hab ihn selig. Er möchte uns offensichtlich etwas mitteilen.

Prinz Albert: Guten Morgen, meine Herren! Ich weiß, wer Sie sind und was Sie hier suchen. Wir Geister besitzen Fähigkeiten, die Sterbliche nicht haben. Ja, genau, ich bin Albert von Sachsen-Coburg und Gotha. Auch nach meinem Tod kümmere ich mich um das Wohl meiner teuren Ehefrau Victoria. Sie möchten wissen, ob Übeltäter ihr Unwesen hier im Palast treiben könnten. Kommen Sie mit, ich zeige Ihnen unseren Palast. Wir nehmen die Tür hier rechts.

Er zeigt auf einen Eingang zwischen zwei Säulen, öffnet die Tür und führt Holmes und Watson durch Räume und an den Stallungen vorbei zum Garten, wo er einen Weg zwischen den Rasenflächen zur Rückseite des Palasts nimmt. Zusammen

of the palace. The three then walk up a few steps to the garden terrace, where Prince Albert stops next to one of the stone urns that adorn the balustrade.

Prince Albert: Perhaps you have never seen the wonderful park hidden behind the palace walls. 40 acres, including the lake. The best view is from the Music Room – the room with windows in a semicircle, up there behind us. I'll take you inside.

He opens a door and guides them through a darkened space to a highly ornate staircase with gilded balustrades beneath a glass dome. They climb the stairs, passing huge portraits. On the upper floor they pass through a long room. Here too paintings hang on the walls, but the works of art are covered by hangings. They then turn left into a large room where the air is stale and dust-sheets have been spread over the furniture.

Prince Albert: The long room was the Picture Gallery, but you can't see the paintings today. We have Rembrandts, of course, and works by Rubens and Vermeer and lots of other old masters. Since I died, Victoria doesn't spend much time here. She feels more at home at Windsor Castle, so the palace is deserted ten months of the year. The rooms are closed und darkened. But I remember what marvellous times we had, especially here in the Music Room. Mendelssohn played for us three times, and Johann Strauss from Vienna was another of our guests. Did you know that I composed music myself?

steigen sie einige Stufen zur Gartenterrasse hinauf. Dort hält Prinz Albert neben der mit steinernen Urnen verzierten Balustrade an.

Prinz Albert: Sie haben diesen herrlichen Park, der sich hinter den Palastmauern verbirgt, möglicherweise noch nie gesehen. 40 Morgen Land zusammen mit dem See. Den besten Blick darauf hat man vom Musiksaal – dort oben hinter uns, von den Fenstern in diesem vorspringenden Halbkreis. Ich nehme Sie mit dorthinein.

Er schließt eine Tür auf und führt sie durch einen abgedunkelten Saal in ein prächtiges Treppenhaus mit vergoldeten Zierbalustraden. Unter einer Glaskuppel steigen sie an riesigen Wandporträts vorbei in die obere Etage. Dann durchschreiten sie ein langes Zimmer. Auch hier hängen Gemälde an den Wänden, aber sie sind mit Stoff abgedeckt. Sie gehen nach links und betreten einen großen Saal. Die Luft ist abgestanden, und schwere Decken sind über die Möbel ausgebreitet.

Prinz Albert: Das lange Zimmer eben war die Picture Gallery, aber die Bilder können Sie heute nicht sehen. Wir besitzen Gemälde von Rembrandt, natürlich, und auch von Rubens, Vermeer und vielen anderen alten Meistern. Seit meinem Tod verbringt Victoria wenig Zeit hier. Sie fühlt sich auf Schloss Windsor wohler, und deshalb ist dieser Palast zehn Monate im Jahr verlassen, die Räume sind abgeschlossen und dunkel. Aber ich erinnere mich an die wunderbaren Zeiten, die wir hier hatten, vor allem in diesem Musiksaal. Dreimal spielte Mendelssohn hier für uns, und auch Johann Strauss aus Wien war zu Gast. Wussten Sie, dass ich selbst komponierte?

Holmes: Your Majesty, of course we are familiar with your artistic accomplishments. However, Dr Watson and I have come with a different matter in mind.

Prince Albert: Patience, Mr Holmes, I'll show you what you want to see. I know the palace better than anyone. When Victoria and I moved in, it was in a terrible state, and I had the job of putting things to rights. Victoria wanted me to keep out of state business, at least in our first years, so I had more than enough time to see to the palace. There was too little accommodation for guests, and no nursery rooms at all. We couldn't heat the place properly because the fireplaces were faulty and filled the rooms with smoke. It was always cold, and what was worse, the whole place stank because it was disgustingly dirty – our servants were too lazy to do the cleaning. Well, I changed all that!

Watson: You are well known, sir, for your good deeds and orderly habits.

Prince Albert: Yes, but that didn't always make me popular. Your English aristocrats thought I was stiff and formal. They didn't trust someone who was more educated than they were, and I had no interest in spending my days hunting foxes. And apart from all that, as they saw it, marriage to the second son of the duke of a small principality in Germany wasn't glorious enough for the monarch of Great Britain and its empire – even though my uncle Leopold had become King of Belgium.

Holmes: You won them all over in the end. The Great Exhibition of 1851 was due to your efforts, and that was one of the greatest events of this century. And thanks to you, the succession to the throne was assured.

Holmes: Selbstverständlich sind uns Ihre musikalischen Leistungen bekannt, Majestät, aber Watson und mich führt ein anderes Anliegen hierher.

Prinz Albert: Nur Geduld, Mr Holmes, ich zeige Ihnen, was Sie sehen möchten. Ich kenne den Palast wie meine Westentasche. Als Victoria und ich nach unserer Hochzeit einzogen, war er in einem furchtbaren Zustand, und es war meine Aufgabe, die Dinge in Ordnung zu bringen. Ich hatte genug Zeit dafür, da Victoria mich zumindest in ihren ersten Regierungsjahren von den Staatsgeschäften fernhalten wollte. Es gab zu wenig Platz für Gäste und gar keine Kinderzimmer. Wir konnten nicht richtig heizen, alle Kamine waren defekt. Die Räume waren voller Rauch, und es war immer kalt. Noch schlimmer war der entsetzliche Dreck – das Personal war faul und putzte nicht richtig. Nun, all das habe ich geändert!

Watson: Sie sind weithin für Ihre guten Taten und Ihren Ordnungssinn bekannt, Sir.

Prinz Albert: Ja, aber das hat mich nicht immer beliebt gemacht. Eure englischen Adligen hielten mich für steif. Sie misstrauten jemandem, der gebildeter war als sie, und ich hatte kein Interesse daran, meine Zeit mit Fuchsjagden zu verbringen. Und davon abgesehen, fanden sie den zweiten Sohn des Herzogs eines deutschen Kleinstaats keine wirklich glanzvolle Partie für die Monarchin des britischen Weltreichs. Obwohl mein Onkel Leopold König von Belgien war!

Holmes: Aber am Ende haben Sie alle überzeugt. Die große Weltausstellung von 1851 war Ihr Werk, eines der bedeutendsten Ereignisse unseres Jahrhunderts. Und dank Ihnen war die Thronfolge gesichert.

Prince Albert: Yes, we had nine children! I knew how to bring them up properly, so they all survived childhood. Six of them married into German royal families. The succession is taken care of, and Victoria has made sure that I will not be forgotten. The Royal Albert Hall was named after me, of course, and opposite they have erected a really imposing monument. It's almost 180 feet high! I'm seated on a throne under a great canopy, surrounded by allegorical figures. And they even gilded me. A most satisfactory commemoration, I must say. I owe it all to Victoria. She has been a widow for 33 years now, and she is still in mourning. She has hot water taken to my bedroom at Windsor Castle every evening, as if I were still alive.

Holmes *(takes his watch from his waistcoat pocket)*: Now if Your Majesty would excuse us …

Prince Albert: Ah yes, why did I bring you here? Look outside. A high wall surrounds the palace grounds. Guards are on patrol even when the court is not present. If I hadn't let you inside, you wouldn't have been able to enter the Royal Mews. The east front is even better guarded. I'll take you there and let you out.

They descend by the magnificent golden staircase, pass through a spacious entrance hall and walk out into the empty inner courtyard, which they cross in order to reach the east wing. Here a dark stairway takes them to the balcony room on the façade that faces The Mall.

Prinz Albert: Ja, neun Kinder haben wir bekommen! Ich wusste, wie man sie richtig großzieht, deshalb haben sie alle die Kindheit überlebt. Sechs davon heirateten in deutsche Fürstenhäuser ein. Die Thronfolge ist gesichert, und Victoria hat dafür gesorgt, dass ich nicht vergessen werde. Die Konzerthalle, die Royal Albert Hall, trägt ja meinen Namen – und gegenüber setzte man mir ein wahrlich beeindruckendes Denkmal. Fast 180 Fuß (54 Meter) hoch! Ich throne unter dem Baldachin, umgeben von allegorischen Figuren. Sogar vergoldet haben sie mich. Mit solch einem Erinnerungszeichen kann man wirklich zufrieden sein. Das habe ich alles Victoria zu verdanken. Seit 33 Jahren ist sie nun schon Witwe, trauert immer noch und lässt jeden Abend heißes Wasser in mein Schlafzimmer im Schloss Windsor bringen, als wäre ich noch am Leben.

Holmes *(holt seine Uhr aus der Westentasche)***:** Wenn Eure Majestät uns nun entschuldigen …

Prinz Albert: Ah genau, warum habe ich Sie gerade hierhin geführt? Schauen Sie hinaus. Eine hohe Mauer umschließt das ganze Gelände. Gardisten patrouillieren auch, wenn der Hof nicht anwesend ist. Hätte ich Sie nicht hereingelassen, wären Sie nie in die Royal Mews gekommen. Die Ostseite des Palasts ist noch besser bewacht. Ich bringe Sie dorthin und lasse Sie wieder hinaus.

Sie steigen das prachtvolle gold verzierte Treppenhaus hinab, gehen durch eine imposante Eingangshalle und treten in den menschenleeren Innenhof. Diesen überqueren sie, um zum Ostflügel zu gelangen. Hier führt eine dunkle Treppe sie in das Balkonzimmer auf der Fassadenseite mit Blick auf The Mall.

Prince Albert: Within ten years the palace was too small for our growing family. Originally a fine triumphal arch stood here. We had to drive through it to enter the courtyard that you have just seen. You know it: Marble Arch. We had it removed to Hyde Park and built this wing of the palace in its place, to enclose the courtyard completely. Which gave us this wonderful view of The Mall and St James's Park from the balcony. It's the ideal grandstand for big occasions. Victoria and I reviewed the troops from here before they went off to the Crimean War. And now look out at the guards: the palace is absolutely secure from this side too. And if some wrong-doer should nevertheless succeed in creeping in, he has to contend with me. I look after this palace!

He leads Holmes and Watson down to the courtyard in front of the palace and takes his leave at the gate. From here Holmes and Watson walk a short distance along The Mall, turn right into St James's Park and take a path that crosses the bridge over the lake. Beyond the bridge they bear left, walk parallel to the lake and leave the park at its south-east corner. Via Great George Street they reach Parliament Square, on the south side of which stands Westminster Abbey.

Prinz Albert: Nach zehn Jahren war der Palast für unsere stetig wachsende Familie zu klein. Hier stand früher ein schöner Triumphbogen, durch den wir hindurchfahren mussten, um zu dem Innenhof zu gelangen, den Sie eben gesehen haben. Ja, genau: Marble Arch. Den Bogen entfernten wir und ließen ihn im Hyde Park aufstellen – und bauten dann diesen neuen Flügel, der den Innenhof komplett umschließt. So bekamen wir vom Balkon aus diesen wunderschönen Blick auf The Mall und St James's Park. Eine perfekte Bühne für große Ereignisse! Von hier aus verabschiedeten Victoria und ich die Truppen in den Krimkrieg. Und schauen Sie auf die Wache: Auch von dieser Seite ist der Palast bestens geschützt. Sollte ein Verbrecher trotzdem hineinschleichen, muss er mit mir rechnen. Ich passe auf den Palast auf!

Er führt Holmes und Watson hinunter zum Vorhof des Palasts, verabschiedet sich am Tor. Von hier aus laufen Holmes und Watson ein Stück The Mall entlang, biegen rechts in den St James's Park und nehmen einen Weg, der über die Brücke am See führt. Nach der Brücke halten sie sich links, gehen parallel zum See und verlassen den Park an der Südostecke. Über die Great George Street kommen sie zum Parliament Square, an dessen Südseite die Westminster Abbey steht.

3.

Coronations and Tombs
(Westminster Abbey)

Krönungen und Gräber
(Westminster Abbey)

With death doomed to grapple,
beneath his cold slab,
he who lied in the chapel
now lies in the abbey.

Lord Byron, epitaph for William Pitt

Westminster Abbey, where coronations have been held since 1066 and 17 monarchs laid to rest, has the status of a national shrine, as a huge number of famous people - statesmen, military men, scientists, artists, writers - have been buried within its walls or honoured by a memorial. The most recent great occasion in Westminster Abbey was the marriage of Prince William to Kate Middleton in April 2011.

The pious King Edward the Confessor founded an abbey on what was once marshy land by the Thames, as he had been unable to fulfil his vow to make a pilgrimage to Rome. He was buried in the unfinished church in 1066. After Edward was declared to have been a saint, pilgrims came to his tomb. This led Henry III to commission the building of a new church in the Gothic style in 1245, but 500 years were to pass before the construction of the abbey came to an end with the completion of the west towers.

The crowds who queue to admire the architecture, royal tombs and memorials to the great and the good pay a steep price for admission to the abbey. In order to avoid the charges, enjoy Westminster Abbey in a more peaceful atmosphere and listen to an excellent choir, it is a good idea to attend Evensong (Mon -

Oder: Vom Tode hinunter gezogen
Unter kalten Marmor und Blei,
Der in der Kapell' einst gelogen,
Er liegt jetzt in der Abtei.

Lord Byron, Grabschrift auf S. Herrl. William Pitt

Westminster Abbey ist Krönungsort seit 1066 und letzte Ruhestätte von 17 Monarchen. Die Kirche ist ein nationales Heiligtum, weil innerhalb der Mauern eine große Anzahl von berühmten Personen – Staatsmänner, Soldaten, Wissenschaftler, Künstler und Schriftsteller – beerdigt sind oder mit einem Denkmal geehrt werden. Das letzte große Ereignis in Westminster Abbey war die Hochzeit von Prinz William und Kate Middleton im April 2011. Der fromme König Edward the Confessor (dt. der Bekenner) gründete eine Abtei auf ehemaligem Sumpfland an der Themse, da er sein Gelübde, nach Rom zu pilgern, nicht einhalten konnte. Er wurde im Jahr 1066 in der unvollendeten Kirche begraben. Nach Edwards Heiligsprechung kamen viele Pilger zu seiner Grabstätte. Das bewegte Henry III. dazu, ab 1245 eine neue Kirche im gotischen Stil zu errichten. Doch es hat 500 Jahre gedauert, bis mit den beiden Westtürmen der Bau der Westminster Abbey vollendet war.

Besucher, die sich in die Schlange stellen, um die Architektur, Königsgräber sowie die Denkmäler für große Berühmtheiten zu bewundern, zahlen einen saftigen Eintrittspreis. Wenn man die Kosten vermeiden möchte, ist es eine gute Idee, den Abendgottesdienst «Evensong» zu besuchen (Mo.-Fr. 17 Uhr, Sa./So. meist 15 Uhr) und

Fri 5 pm, Sat – Sun usually 3 pm), although there is
then no opportunity to explore the church.

Holmes and Watson cross Parliament Square and enter
Westminster Abbey through the north door. Inside the
church it is cooler and quieter than on the busy, sunny
square. The footsteps and low voices of unseen persons
echo high in the vaults, but the man who approaches
them seems to glide silently over the stone slabs of the
floor. He is dressed in a long coat, a waistcoat, and
breeches of fine, red-brown velvet, wears a white shoul-
der-length wig and has a double chin and a high forehead.

Watson: Well, Holmes, who is this coming to greet us?
Do you think it's another ghost?

Holmes: It seems so, and I'm glad of it. There's no better
way of getting to know the abbey. This is clearly a composer – look, he's holding sheets of music.

Composer: You are wondering who I am. Perhaps you'll
recognise this: "I know tha-at my redee-eemer liveth."

Holmes: An excerpt from *The Messiah*, of course. So
you are George Frederic Handel. If I'm not mistaken,
your grave is here in the abbey.

Handel: I'll show you. It's over there, surrounded by po-
ets and writers.

They walk across the church, passing the high altar on the
left and the choir stalls on the right. Handel stops in the
south transept and points to a monument on the right.

Handel: An excellent memorial, as I'm sure you'll
agree. The sculptor was the best in all England in
my time – Roubiliac was his name. It's rather a good

Westminster Abbey in einer friedlichen Atmosphäre und
bei hervorragendem Chorgesang zu genießen

Holmes und Watson überqueren Parliament Square und betreten die Westminster Abbey durch das Nordportal. Drinnen ist es kühler und stiller ist als auf dem geschäftigen, son-
nigen Platz. Fußtritte und gedämpfte Stimmen unsichtbarer
Personen hallen lange im hohen Gewölbe, doch der Mann,
der auf sie zukommt, scheint lautlos über den Steinboden zu
gleiten. Er ist in Rock, Weste und Kniehosenaus rotbraunem
Samt gekleidet, trägt eine schulterlange weiße Perücke, hat
ein Doppelkinn und eine hohe Stirn.

Watson: Wer uns da wohl begrüßen kommt, Holmes? Meinen
   Sie, dass es ein weiterer Geist ist?
Holmes: Es sieht zum Glück ganz danach aus. Es gibt keine
   bessere Art, die Kirche kennenzulernen. Dies ist zweifellos
   ein Komponist. Sehen Sie, er hält eine Partitur in der Hand.
Komponist: Sie fragen sich, wer ich bin. Vielleicht erkennen
   Sie dieses Stück: «Ich weiß, da-ass mein Erlö-öser lebet.»
Holmes: Natürlich, das ist aus ‹Der Messias›! Sie sind also
   Georg Friedrich Händel. Wenn ich mich nicht irre, befindet
   sich Ihr Grab hier in Westminster Abbey.
Händel: Ich zeige es Ihnen. Dort drüben, von Dichtern und
   Schriftstellern umringt.

Sie durchqueren die Kirche, links an dem Hochaltar, rechts
an dem Chorgestühl vorbei. Händel bleibt im südlichen Querschiff stehen und zeigt auf ein Denkmal auf der rechten Seite.

Händel: Ein würdiges Grabmal, nicht wahr? Der Bildhauer
   war der beste in ganz England zu meiner Zeit – Roubiliac
   hieß er. Er hat mich ziemlich gut getroffen. Und schauen

likeness. And look, in the background he carved an organ, and there is King David with his harp, and I'm holding this music.

Watson: How do you feel with all these writers around you? I can see a lot of famous names: Jane Austen, Lord Byron, Charles Dickens, Shakespeare, Wordsworth …

Handel: Fitting company, on the whole, apart from that scandalous rake Byron. If you ask me, the actor Garrick got the best memorial in this part of the abbey. Do you see the dramatic way he's holding those stage curtains apart to take his last bow? Of course, most of the people who are commemorated here just got a plaque or a monument, and they are buried somewhere else. But Dickens' grave really is here, and so is mine – and I have strong links to Westminster Abbey. Do you know my coronation music?

Watson: Whose coronation did you compose for?

Handel: For George II. I held the post of master of music for his father, George I, who was still Elector of Hanover at the time and not yet King of England. It was for George I and his guests that I wrote the *Water Music*. We performed it in boats on the Thames. And I remember his son's coronation as if it were yesterday. Poor George II, he was so hot under his heavy fur-lined robes that he fainted. We could almost have crowned and buried him on the same day. But my music went down extremely well. I wrote four anthems, and one of them, *Zadok the Priest*, has been played at every coronation since.

Watson: There must have been many solemn funeral services here, too.

Sie, im Hintergrund hat er eine Orgel gemeißelt, und dort ist König David mit Harfe, und in meiner Hand halte ich diese Partitur.

Watson: Wie fühlen Sie sich in der Gesellschaft dieser ganzen Schriftsteller? Ich sehe viele bekannte Namen: Jane Austen, Charles Dickens, Lord Byron, Shakespeare, Wordsworth …

Händel: Alles in allem keine schlechte Gesellschaft, bis auf den Wüstling Byron. Das beste Denkmal hat in diesem Teil der Kirche meines Erachtens der Schauspieler Garrick. Schauen Sie, wie dramatisch er die Vorhänge auseinanderhält, um sich ein letztes Mal zu verbeugen? Die meisten bekamen hier natürlich nur ein Denkmal oder eine Tafel mit Inschrift und sind woanders beerdigt. Aber Dickens' Grab ist tatsächlich hier, meins auch – und mich verbindet viel mit der Westminster Abbey. Kennen Sie meine Krönungsmusik?

Watson: Für wessen Krönung komponierten Sie?

Händel: Für George II. Ich war Kapellmeister seines Vaters, George I., als er Kurfürst von Hannover und noch nicht König von England war. Für ihn und seine Gäste schrieb ich die ‹Wassermusik›, die wir in Booten auf der Themse aufführten. An die Krönung seines Sohnes erinnere ich mich, als wäre es gestern gewesen. Unter den schweren Pelzen schwitzte er so sehr, dass er in Ohnmacht fiel. Beinahe hätten wir ihn am selben Tag krönen und beerdigen können. Meine Musik aber war ein voller Erfolg! Vier Hymnen schrieb ich. Eine davon, ‹Zadok the Priest›, wurde seitdem bei jeder Krönung gespielt.

Watson: Hier gab es sicherlich auch viele feierliche Begräbnisse.

Handel: Certainly. My own, for example. I had asked for a private burial, but they made it almost a state occasion, and I won't complain about that. 3000 people came to mourn me, and three choirs sang. Only monarchs are buried with more pomp. Of course kings get the best places and the most expensive graves. Would you like to see them?

He leads them to the eastern part of the church, passing the shrine of Edward the Confessor, around which are the tombs of four medieval kings.

Handel: Take a look at these kings from the old days. That beautiful bronze figure up there is Henry III, who ordered the building of this church. And there is his successor, Edward I. A big tomb, but without an effigy because there was no money left. King Edward had spent all his treasure fighting the Scots.

Holmes: On that subject: perhaps you could point out the grave of Mary, Queen of Scots?

Handel: But of course. We are on the way to the Chapel of Henry VII, and that's where I shall leave you.

From 1502 one of the greatest achievements of English architecture was built at the east end of the abbey: the Lady Chapel, also known as Henry VII's Chapel. The first monarch of the House of Tudor ordered its construction as a royal mausoleum and, although in other respects he was a thrifty king, he spared no expense on the chapel. Its fan vault with lace-like patterns seems to defy gravity and is the consummation

Händel: Gewiss! Mein eigenes, zum Beispiel. Ich hatte um eine private Beerdigung gebeten, aber sie wurde fast zu einem Staatsakt. 3000 Menschen kamen, um mich zu betrauern, drei Chöre sangen. Nur Könige werden mit mehr Glanz und Gloria zu Grabe getragen. Monarchen bekommen natürlich die teuersten Grabmäler und die besten Plätze. Möchten Sie die Gräber sehen?

Händel führt sie zum Ostteil der Kirche am Schrein von Edward the Confessor vorbei. Um ihn herum befinden sich die Hochgräber von vier Königen aus dem Mittelalter.

Händel: Werfen Sie einen Blick auf die alten Könige. Die schöne Bronzefigur dort oben ist Henry III., der den Neubau der Kirche veranlasste. Dort ist sein Nachfolger, Edward I. Das Grab ist groß, aber ohne eine Statue: Es gab kein Geld mehr, er hatte alles für Kriege gegen die Schotten ausgegeben.

Holmes: Da Sie Schottland erwähnen: Können Sie uns vielleicht das Grab von Maria Stuart zeigen?

Händel: Selbstverständlich. Wir sind auf dem Weg zur Kapelle von Henry VII., und dort werde ich Sie verlassen.

Ab 1502 entstand im Osten eines der Glanzstücke englischer Architektur: die Marienkapelle, auch Kapelle von Henry VII. genannt. Dieser erste Monarch der Tudor-Dynastie ließ sie als königliches Mausoleum bauen und sparte bei der Ausführung an nichts, obwohl er ansonsten ein knauseriger Herrscher war. Das fächerförmige Deckengewölbe mit den spitzenartig angeordneten Steinen scheint der Schwerkraft zu trotzen

of the Perpendicular style, the last phase of Gothic
architecture in England.

Handel points to a grave in the south aisle of the
chapel. A marble figure depicts a recumbent woman,
her hands joined in prayer. The details of her elaborate
collar and fur-lined robe have been exquisitely carved.
Her head rests on a decorated pillow; a crowned Scottish lion lies at her feet. Holmes and Watson, admir-
ing the sculptor's skill, fail to notice that Handel
has disappeared and a female figure has taken his
place.

Mary, Queen of Scots: My son commissioned this tomb.
In the end honour was satisfied – better late than never.

Holmes and Watson turn, startled, when she speaks and
note the similarity between her and the effigy on the
tomb.

Mary, Queen of Scots: I'm sure you know my story.
Don't you? Queen of Scotland when I was six days
old, later Queen of France. By the age of 17 I was a
widow, and back in Scotland. You can hardly imagine what things were like there! Intrigues and plots
on all sides, noble families at daggers drawn. I was
surrounded by vipers and traitors – and, even worse,
moralising Puritans. The worst of them all was John
Knox. They called him a "reformer". What a terrible man! He dared to preach and rant at me about
how I should behave. I admit, my choice of hus-
bands could have been better, but a queen's subjects
should know their place and not pass judgement

und ist eine Vollendung des «Perpendicular»-Stils, der letzten Phase der gotischen Architektur in England.

Händel weist auf ein Grab im rechten Seitenschiff. Die marmorne Figur einer liegenden Frau hält die Hände zum Gebet gefaltet. Feine Details ihrer kostbaren Halskrause und eines pelzgefütterten Mantels sind fein differenziert gemeißelt. Ihr Kopf ruht auf einem verzierten Kissen, zu ihren Füßen liegt ein gekrönter schottischer Löwe. Holmes und Watson bewundern das Geschick des Bildhauers und merken nicht, dass Händel verschwunden ist und eine weibliche Figur seinen Platz eingenommen hat.

Maria Stuart: Mein Sohn hat das Grab in Auftrag gegeben. Meine Ehre wurde wiederhergestellt – besser spät als nie!

Holmes und Watson drehen sich erschrocken um und stellen die Ähnlichkeit ihrer Erscheinung mit der Figur auf dem Grabmal fest.

Maria Stuart: Meine Geschichte kennen Sie sicher. Nein? Im Alter von sechs Tagen wurde ich Königin von Schottland, später Königin von Frankreich. Mit 17 Jahren war ich bereits Witwe und zurück in Schottland. Sie können sich nicht vorstellen, was für Zustände dort herrschten! Intrigen und Verschwörungen auf allen Seiten, Adelshäuser auf Kriegsfuß miteinander. Giftschlangen und Verräter umringten mich – und schlimmer noch, Moralisten und Puritaner. Der Schrecklichste von allen war John Knox. Einen «Reformator» nannte man ihn. Solch ein furchtbarer Mann! Er wagte es, mir Predigten zu halten und mich abzukanzeln – zugegeben, meine Ehemänner waren nicht gut gewählt, aber ein Untertan hat nicht über den Lebenswandel seiner

on her morals. When everyone turned against me I had no choice but to flee to England …

Holmes: … where Elizabeth I put you under arrest.

Mary, Queen of Scots: My royal cousin kept me prisoner for 18 years. In all that time I never gave up my claim to the English throne, which is why Elizabeth put me on trial and signed my death warrant. She didn't even have the decency to pay for a good executioner. It took him three swipes of the axe to cut off my head.

Holmes: However, you said that honour was satisfied in the end.

Mary, Queen of Scots: O yes, the House of Stuart had the last laugh. I bore a son, while Elizabeth remained childless. So my son James ruled both Scotland and England, and our family burial vault here in the abbey is full of later generations of the Stuart dynasty who ruled north and south of the border.

Watson: In that case we are all the more honoured to avert the dangers that threaten this church. This is the task that has brought us to Westminster Abbey.

Mary, Queen of Scots: If you need assistance in protecting the abbey, then I can take you to the right person.

She leads the way around the royal chapel, past the tomb of her rival Elizabeth I, and proceeds to the north transept, where Holmes and Watson entered. There she points to a large tomb on the eastern wall in the second, rear row of monuments, where a dramatic scene is depicted. Death, shown as a half-veiled skeleton, creeps out of a

Königin zu urteilen! Als alle gegen mich waren, hatte ich keine andere Wahl, als nach England zu fliehen …

Holmes: …wo Königin Elizabeth I. Sie inhaftierte.

Maria Stuart: 18 Jahre hat mich meine königliche Cousine in Gefangenschaft gehalten. Weil ich mich standhaft weigerte, meinen Anspruch auf den englischen Thron aufzugeben, machte mir Elizabeth den Prozess und unterschrieb mein Todesurteil. Sie hatte nicht einmal den Anstand, für einen gescheiten Henker zu zahlen. Drei Axtschläge brauchte der Mann, um mich zu enthaupten.

Holmes: Aber Sie erwähnten, dass Ihre Ehre zuletzt doch wiederhergestellt wurde.

Maria Stuart: In der Tat, am Ende triumphierte das Haus Stuart. Ich hatte einen Sohn, Elizabeth blieb kinderlos. Also regierte mein Sohn James sowohl Schottland als auch England, und unsere Familiengruft in dieser Kirche ist mit späteren Generationen aus dem Hause Stuart, die nördlich und südlich der Grenze herrschten, voll besetzt.

Watson: Dann ist es für uns eine besondere Ehre, jegliche Gefahr, die dieser Kirche droht, abzuwehren. Das ist der Auftrag, der uns in die Westminster Abbey gebracht hat.

Maria Stuart: Wenn Sie beim Beschützen der Kirche Unterstützung brauchen, kann ich Sie mit der richtigen Person bekannt machen.

Sie führt um die königliche Kapelle herum, am Grab ihrer Rivalin Elizabeth I. vorbei, geht dann ins nördliche Querschiff, wo Holmes und Watson die Kirche betreten haben. Dort zeigt sie auf ein großes Grab in zweiter Reihe an der östlichen Seite, auf dem eine dramatische Szene dargestellt ist. Der Tod, als Skelett personifiziert und halb verschleiert, schleicht aus

grave and aims a dart at a woman above who is shrinking back, seeking support on the shoulder of a man. While Holmes and Watson take in this sight, Mary, Queen of Scots vanishes. A moment later a pale woman in a long silk dress has appeared in front of the monument.

Pale woman: Come over here! Now! You're looking for the man who was snooping in the abbey yesterday. He was poking around my memorial, from top to bottom. I had the impression that he wanted to hide something in it or underneath it.

Holmes *(examines the inscription)*: You are Elizabeth Nightingale, I presume. Please accept my condolences on your early death. I suppose that's your husband who is shielding you with his hand.

Elizabeth Nightingale: Your condolences are no more use to me than the weak protection that my husband offered, Mr Holmes.

Watson: Did you really meet such a terrible end as this scene here suggests?

Elizabeth Nightingale: I was out walking, eight months pregnant. A bolt of lightning struck right next to me without warning and split a huge oak tree by the wayside. The shock brought on a premature birth. The child survived, but I died in frightful pain. And as for all these sculptural histrionics that you see, that was my brother-in-law's idea. He once had a bad dream, like the anxious, quaking fellow he was. He thought a skeleton had crept into his bed and was snuggling up to my sister. This memorial that you see here was the result of his pathetic fantasies.

einer Gruft und zielt mit einem Pfeil auf eine Frau, die zurückfällt und Halt an der Schulter eines Mannes sucht. Während Holmes und Watson den Anblick auf sich wirken lassen, verschwindet Maria Stuart. Kurz darauf steht eine blasse Dame in einem langen Seidenkleid vor dem Grabmal.

Blasse Dame: Kommen Sie her! Sofort! Sie suchen den Mann, der gestern in der Abtei herumschnüffelte. Er hat mein Grabmal von oben bis unten inspiziert. Es sah aus, als wollte er etwas darin oder darunter verstecken.

Holmes *(blickt auf die Inschrift)*: Ich nehme an, Sie sind Elizabeth Nightingale. Darf ich mein Bedauern über Ihren frühen Tod ausdrücken? Das ist vermutlich Ihr Ehemann, der eine schützende Hand ausstreckt.

Elizabeth Nightingale: Ihr Bedauern nutzt mir so wenig wie damals der schwache Schutz meines Mannes, Mr Holmes.

Watson: Erlitten Sie tatsächlich einen so schrecklichen Tod, wie diese Darstellung nahelegt?

Elizabeth Nightingale: Ich war im achten Monat schwanger und spazieren, als ein gewaltiger Blitz ohne jede Vorwarnung neben mir einschlug und eine mächtige Eiche am Wegesrand spaltete. Der Schreck führte zu einer Frühgeburt. Das Kind überlebte, ich starb unter großen Schmerzen. Und was dieses theatralische Bildhauerwerk betrifft: Die Idee stammte von meinem Schwager. Er war ein ängstlicher, immer in seinen Stiefeln zitternder Mann und hatte einmal einen Albtraum: Er träumte, dass ein Skelett in sein Bett kroch und sich an meine Schwester kuschelte. Das Denkmal, das Sie hier sehen, ist das Resultat seiner er-

When a sculptor takes up his chisel, it's always the same story: men are valiant, women are weak. Look at it: my brave husband holds out his hand, and I swoon against him. What a falsehood! I've frightened men away more than once. Everyone knows the story of how a thief sneaked into the abbey one night, saw this skeleton with its dart in the moonlight, and ran away in terror. The crowbar that he left behind was on show for many years. But the truth is that I drove him off – and if that good-for-nothing who was here yesterday shows his ugly thin face here again …

Watson: Bravo! You will protect the abbey, this wonderful symbol of the might of our empire! We don't know exactly what that man is threatening to do, but perhaps foreign anarchists are plotting an attack.

Elizabeth Nightingale: I've no time for that kind of hollow patriotism. Look around you: foreigners were at work everywhere in this church. My memorial, like Handel's, was the work of Monsieur Roubiliac – now does that sound like an English name? The best sculptor in London in my lifetime? – a Frenchman. The outstanding composer? – a German. Did you see the magnificent mosaic by the high altar? That is called a Cosmati pavement. It was done 600 years ago by craftsmen from Rome. Not to mention the royal tombs. The effigy of Henry VII was made by Pietro Torrigiani, because no Englishman could cast bronze as well as he could. The figures of Henry's mother and his queen were also by Torrigiani.

Watson: So you do admit that women, too, are honoured in this church.

bärmlichen Hirngespinste. Wenn Bildhauer ihre Meißel in die Hand nehmen, ist es immer das gleiche Lied: Männer sind tapfer, Frauen sind schwach. Schauen Sie hin: Mein Mann ist tapfer, hält mir seine Hand hin, und ich falle ihm in die Arme. Das ist gelogen! Ich habe Männer mehr als einmal in die Flucht geschlagen. Alle kennen die Geschichte, wie ein Dieb nachts in die Westminster Abbey einbrach, das Gerippe mit Pfeil im Mondschein sah und davonlief. Das Brecheisen, das er hinterließ, wurde lange Zeit ausgestellt. Aber in Wahrheit war ich es, die ihn vertrieb – und wenn dieser Taugenichts von gestern noch einmal sein hässliches, dünnes Gesicht zeigt …

Watson: Bravo! Sie werden unsere Kirche, dieses Symbol des britischen Weltreichs, beschützen! Wir wissen nicht genau, was der Mann zu tun droht, aber vielleicht planen ausländische Anarchisten einen Anschlag.

Elizabeth Nightingale: Jetzt ersparen Sie mir diesen hohlen Patriotismus. Blicken Sie sich um: Hier waren Ausländer überall am Werk. Auch mein Grabmal, wie das von Händel, ist das Werk von Roubiliac – klingt der Name etwa englisch? Der beste Bildhauer meiner Zeit in London? – ein Franzose. Der herausragende Komponist? – ein Deutscher. Und haben Sie das prachtvolle Mosaik am Hauptaltar gesehen? Einen Cosmati-Fußboden nennt man das. Er wurde vor 600 Jahren von Meistern aus Rom gefertigt. Von den Königsgräbern ganz zu schweigen. Die Figur von Henry VII. ist von Pietro Torrigiani, weil kein Engländer damals so gut Bronze gießen konnte. Auch die Figuren von Henrys Mutter und seiner Königin stammen von Torrigiani.

Watson: Also müssen Sie zugeben, dass auch Frauen in dieser Kirche geehrt werden.

Elizabeth Nightingale: And how are they honoured? Take a good look at the grave of the Countess of Lennox. She was laid to rest in Henry VII's Chapel. Like me she has all the solace of a fine tomb, as well as the company of her eight children, who are depicted as weepers, mourning for her. But the truth was, it was the other way round: the mother grieved for her children, because six of them died in childhood and she outlived the other two. That's the fate of women – while the men boast about their great deeds.

She points to the statues in the Statesmen's Aisle opposite, where generals and admirals dressed in fine uniforms and politicians strike heroic poses, declaim or gaze resolutely into the distance.

Holmes: You have given us our cue, Mrs Nightingale. It's time for us to go to the Houses of Parliament.

Elizabeth Nightingale: The place where self-important gentlemen make interminable speeches! Be gone, and leave the abbey to the women. We'll keep it safe from intruders.

Elizabeth Nightingale: Aber wie werden wir geehrt? Sehen
   Sie sich das Grab der Countess of Lennox (dt. Gräfin von
   Lennox) einmal genau an – sie liegt in der Henry VII. Chapel. Wie ich genießt sie den Trost eines schönen Grabmals
   und ist außerdem in Begleitung ihrer acht Kinder, alle als
   weinende Trauerfiguren abgebildet sind. In Wahrheit aber
   war es umgekehrt – die Mutter musste um ihre Kinder
   trauern. Sechs starben im Kindesalter, und Margaret überlebte auch die anderen zwei. Das ist das Los der Frauen,
   während die Männer sich ihrer großen Taten rühmen.

Sie zeigt auf die Denkmäler gegenüber in der Statemen's
Aisle, wo Politiker, in edle Uniformen gekleidete Feldherren
und Admirale heroische Posen einnehmen, deklamieren oder
entschlossen in die Ferne blicken.

Holmes: Sie geben mir das Stichwort, Mrs Nightingale. Wir
   müssen uns auf den Weg zu den Houses of Parliament machen.
Elizabeth Nightingale: Dort, wo die Wichtigtuer endlose Reden halten! Dann gehen Sie und lassen Sie die Kirche in
   den Händen der Frauen. Wir werden sie vor Eindringlingen
   schützen.

4.

Gunpowder, Treason and Fists
(Houses of Parliament)

Schießpulver, Hochverrat
und Fausthiebe
(Houses of Parliament)

Remember, remember, the fifth of November,
Gunpowder, treason and plot.
I see no reason why gunpowder treason
Should ever be forgot.

Traditional rhyme

The complex of buildings used by Parliament is named the Palace of Westminster because it was the site of the royal court from the time of Edward the Confessor. Westminster Hall is the remaining part of the medieval palace. When it was built in 1099 it was the largest hall in Europe, and three centuries later Henry Yevele, architect of Westminster Abbey, added the magnificent hammer-beam roof, which spans a space measuring 21 by 73 metres without intermediate supports. Westminster Hall was the scene of coronation banquets and some of the most noteworthy trials in the history of England. Today it is used on exceptional occasions before funerals, as the place where the deceased lies in state while the public pay their respects: in 1965 for Sir Winston Churchill, in 2002 for the Queen Mother.

To reach the Palace of Westminster Holmes and Watson turn right when leaving Westminster Abbey and walk past St Margaret's Church. Across the road Westminster Hall is directly in front of them, and to their right two elaborately decorated turrets flank the entrance to Parliament.

A tall man with long, reddish-brown hair and a flowing beard approaches them. He is wearing a broadbrimmed hat and a black cloak.

Remember, remember the fifth of November,
Gunpowder, treason and plot!
I see no reason why gunpowder treason
Should ever be forgot.

Traditioneller Reim

Der Gebäudekomplex des Parlaments heißt Palace of Westminster, weil Könige seit Edward the Confessor hier Hof hielten. Der verbliebene Teil des mittelalterlichen Palasts ist Westminster Hall, die im Jahre 1099 als damals größte Halle Europas fertiggestellt wurde. 300 Jahre später baute Henry Yevele, Architekt von Westminster Abbey, die prächtige Stichbalkendecke, die ohne Stützen einen 21 mal 73 Meter großen Raum überspannt. Westminster Hall war die Kulisse für Krönungsbankette und einige der aufsehenerregendsten Gerichtsprozesse. Heute werden hier führende Persönlichkeiten des Königreichs vor der Beerdigung aufgebahrt, damit die Öffentlichkeit die letzte Ehre erweisen kann – im Jahr 1965 Sir Winston Churchill, 2002 Queen Mum.

Holmes und Watson gehen nach Verlassen der Westminster Abbey nach rechts, an der St Margaret's Church vorbei, und überqueren die Straße, um zum Palace of Westminster zu gelangen. Vor ihnen steht die Westminster Hall, auf der rechten Seite flankieren zwei reich geschmückte Türmchen den Eingang zum Parlament.

Ein hochgewachsener Mann mit langen rotbraunen Haaren und einem üppigen Kinnbart kommt auf sie zu. Er trägt einen breitkrempigen Hut und einen schwarzen Umhang.

Bearded man: I see you are taking a close look at the old hall. Perhaps I can help you. Are you looking for the entrance to the cellars?

Holmes *(examines the man's appearance and thinks for a moment)*: Guy Fawkes? Thank you, we would certainly like to look at the cellars. But times have changed, Mr Fawkes. There is no good reason any more for a Catholic conspiracy against the Crown. Catholics have been members of Parliament for more than 60 years. We have come to protect the Palace of Westminster, not to blow it up as you wanted to do.

Guy Fawkes: I was fighting for a righteous cause. In the days of Queen Elizabeth we had to celebrate holy mass in secret and hide our priests. If they were discovered, they were tortured and executed as enemies of the state. If we failed to attend the services of the Anglican church we were forced to pay fines, and those who refused to pay had their property confiscated and were even imprisoned. And then the Scottish king James Stuart succeeded to the throne. We hoped he would allow us to practise the true faith, but he disappointed us – and so we were forced to take action.

Watson: And you failed utterly.

Guy Fawkes: Certainly not! We had a good plan, and it was nearly successful. We rented the cellar below the House of Lords. That was quite normal – lots of people used cellars here for storage space, and we could come and go more or less as we pleased. We brought in 36 tons of gunpowder in barrels and concealed it beneath firewood. That would have been more than enough to send King James straight to hell, and all the members of Par-

Bärtiger Mann: Aha! Sie schauen sich die alte Halle genau an. Vielleicht kann ich Ihnen helfen. Suchen Sie den Eingang zum Keller?

Holmes *(nimmt den Mann in Augenschein und überlegt kurz)*: Guy Fawkes? Vielen Dank, die Kellerräume würden wir in der Tat gerne inspizieren. Aber, Mr Fawkes, die Zeiten haben sich geändert. Es gibt keinen guten Grund mehr für eine katholische Verschwörung gegen die Krone. Seit mehr als 60 Jahren werden Katholiken ins Parlament gewählt. Wir sind gekommen, um den Palace of Westminster zu schützen – nicht, wie Sie damals, um ihn in die Luft zu sprengen.

Guy Fawkes: Ich kämpfte für eine gerechte Sache. In der Zeit von Königin Elizabeth mussten wir die Heilige Messe heimlich feiern und unsere Priester verstecken. Fand man sie doch, wurden sie gefoltert und als Staatsverräter hingerichtet. Wer nicht zum anglikanischen Gottesdienst erschien, musste Strafe zahlen. Wenn man sich weigerte, wurde man enteignet, sogar ins Gefängnis gesteckt. Dann kam der Schotte James Stuart auf den Thron. Wir hatten die Hoffnung, er würde uns die Ausübung des wahren Glaubens erlauben. Aber er hat uns enttäuscht; und wir mussten handeln.

Watson: Und Sie sind kläglich gescheitert.

Guy Fawkes: Ganz und gar nicht! Der Plan war gut und beinahe erfolgreich. Wir pachteten den Keller unterhalb des House of Lords. Das war nicht auffällig: Viele Leute mieteten sich hier Keller als Lagerräume, und wir konnten mehr oder weniger kommen und gehen, wie wir wollten. Wir brachten 36 Tonnen Schießpulver hierher und versteckten sie unter Brennholz – mehr als genug, um König James und alle Parlamentsmitglieder in die Hölle zu schicken. Die

liament with him. We had planned our next moves carefully. A group of trustworthy men were ready and waiting – they were going to take the king's daughter into their custody and put her on the throne. My task was to light the fuse for the detonation and escape across the river. Then I was to round up support in France and Spain for a Roman Catholic monarchy here in England.

Watson: Thank heavens your conspiracy was discovered!

Guy Fawkes: That was only because we weren't ruthless enough. Despite all the persecution, more than a few members of the House of Lords had kept faith with the old religion – discreetly, of course. And one of our number had qualms. He decided to warn the Catholic lords to stay away from the opening of Parliament. His letter fell into the hands of royal ministers, and they ordered a search on the evening before the ceremony. They found me here with the gunpowder.

Holmes: That was almost 300 years ago, and you're still here.

Guy Fawkes: Where else would I be? I was put on trial in this place – here, in Westminster Hall, where many brave men were given the death sentence. Before my time the Scottish rebel William Wallace was condemned here. And Thomas More, who stood by his Catholic faith and steadfastly denied that the king can be head of the Church. So I'm in good company. This is also the place of my execution: New Palace Yard, over there at the end of Westminster Hall. I hurled myself from the scaffold and broke my neck, and so I was no longer alive when the executioner quartered me and pulled my bowels from my belly.

nächsten Schritte hatten wir sorgfältig geplant. Eine Gruppe zuverlässiger Männer stand bereit, die Tochter des Königs in ihre Gewalt zu bringen und auf den Thron zu setzen. Meine Aufgabe war es, die Lunte zu zünden und über die Themse zu entkommen. Dann sollte ich in Spanien und Frankreich um Unterstützung für ein römisch-katholisches Königreich werben.

Watson: Ihre Verschwörung flog aber auf, Gott sei Dank!

Guy Fawkes: Allerdings nur, weil wir nicht skrupellos genug waren. Trotz der ganzen Verfolgung waren etliche Mitglieder des House of Lords der alten Religion treu geblieben – auf diskrete Art und Weise, versteht sich. Einer in unseren Reihen war zu zimperlich. Er wollte die katholischen Lords warnen, damit sie der Eröffnung des Parlaments fernblieben. Sein Schreiben fiel in die Hände der königlichen Minister, und am Abend vor der Feier ließen sie das Gelände durchsuchen. Dort fanden sie mich mit dem Schießpulver.

Holmes: Das war vor fast 300 Jahren, und Sie sind noch immer hier.

Guy Fawkes: Wo sonst? An diesem Ort hat man mich vor Gericht gestellt. Ja, hier, in Westminster Hall, wo vielen mutigen Männern der Prozess gemacht wurde. Vor mir wurde der schottische Rebell William Wallace verurteilt und Thomas More, der an seinem katholischen Glauben festhielt und sich standhaft weigerte, den König als Oberhaupt der Kirche anzuerkennen. Ich bin also in bester Gesellschaft. Hier bin ich auch hingerichtet worden, im New Palace Yard, dort drüben am anderen Ende von Westminster Hall. Ich warf mich vom Schafott und brach mir das Genick. So lebte ich nicht mehr, als der Henker mich vierteilte und mir die Eingeweide aus dem Leib riss.

Holmes: No-one would say that you escaped your just punishment. You live on in the memory of all Englishmen as an evil-doer, and every year your effigy is burnt on a bonfire.

Guy Fawkes: And I'm proud of it. Who knows to-day what King James did? Whereas I made my mark. To this day the Yeomen of the Guard search the cellars of Parliament before the official open-ing.

Holmes: That's no more than a quaint tradition, a ceremony in historical uniforms. Let's forget the bad old days when Catholics were persecuted. Would you be so good as to show us the entrance to the cellars? Did anyone come here yesterday with the same intention – a tall, thin man with a black beard?

Guy Fawkes: You can expect no help from me! But if the one who was here yesterday comes again, I'll give him all the assistance I can. 60 years ago I had the pleasure of watching Parliament burn. If it's destroyed again, I'll cheer.

Holmes and Watson turn their backs on the unre-pentant ghost and walk past New Palace Yard to the corner of the street, where they turn right towards Westminster Bridge and Big Ben.

In 1834 flames engulfed Parliament, and spared al-most no part of the builings except Westminster Hall. The painter J.M.W. Turner captured on his canvas the dramatic scene of the burning Palace of Westminster and the sky lit up by flames. From the south bank of

Holmes: Niemand würde behaupten, dass Sie Ihrer gerechten Strafe entkommen sind. Sie sind für immer als Übeltäter ins Gedächtnis aller Engländer gebrannt und kommen als Strohpuppe jedes Jahr auf den Scheiterhaufen.

Guy Fawkes: Und ich bin stolz darauf. Wer weiß heute noch, was König James in seinem Leben vollbrachte? Ich dagegen habe Spuren hinterlassen. Bis heute durchsucht die königliche Garde die Kellerräume des Parlaments vor der jährlichen Eröffnung.

Holmes: Das ist bloß eine hübsche Tradition, eine Zeremonie in historischen Uniformen. Vergessen wir lieber die schlechten alten Zeiten, in denen Katholiken verfolgt wurden. Würden Sie uns bitte den Kellereingang zeigen? Hat gestern schon jemand danach gefragt – ein großer, dünner Mann mit einem Bart etwa?

Guy Fawkes: Erwarten Sie keine Unterstützung von mir! Wenn der Mann von gestern noch einmal kommt, dann helfe ich ihm mit allen Kräften. Vor 60 Jahren hatte ich schon die Genugtuung zu sehen, wie das Parlament abbrannte. Ich werde jubeln, wenn es wieder zerstört wird.

Holmes und Watson wenden sich von diesem uneinsichtigen Geist ab, gehen am New Palace Yard vorbei bis zur Ecke der Straße, dann rechts in Richtung Westminster Bridge und bleiben vor dem Big Ben stehen.

1834 stand das Parlament in Flammen, es wurde bis auf Westminster Hall kaum eines der Gebäude verschont. Der Maler William Turner hielt das Spektakel des brennenden Palace of Westminster und des von Flammen erleuchteten Himmels auf Leinwand fest. Vom Südufer der Themse, wo

the Thames, where Turner set up his easel, there is a superb view of the Houses of Parliament as they were rebuilt between 1839 and 1888, in the Gothic Revival style for the sake of harmony with Westminster Abbey. Behind the river façade, which is 266 metres long, lie 1100 rooms, including the sumptuously decorated chamber of the House of Lords with its lavish gilding and seats covered in red leather, the much plainer, surprisingly small chamber of the House of Commons. The most recognisable feature of the ensemble is the 88-metre-high clock tower: Big Ben. The clock face is eight metres high, and its minute hand is four metres in length.

Holmes: Someone is waiting for us over there, and I like him a lot more than the traitor Fawkes. As you know, Watson, I'm a keen boxer, but here is an opponent that I wouldn't care to take on. His name is Ben Caunt.

Holmes points to a giant of a man. The tight fit of his breeches reveals that he has thighs like tree trunks to match his muscular torso. His chin is pugnaciously thrust forward, but he has a friendly grin beneath a broad boxer's nose.

Holmes: Ben, good day to you. This is Dr Watson. Perhaps you would tell him your story.

Ben Caunt: I was heavyweight champion of England. That's a long time ago now, but I'll wager that no-one who ever saw one of my fights has forgotten me. My last bout, when I was over 40 years old, went to 60 rounds.

Turner seine Staffelei aufstellte, hat man einen herrlichen Blick auf die neuen Parlamentsgebäude, die zwischen 1839 und 1888 erbaut wurden – im neugotischen Stil, damit sie mit der Architektur der Westminster Abbey harmonieren. Hinter der 266 Meter langen Fassade der Flussseite verbergen sich mehr als 1100 Räume, darunter die prunkvoll ausgestattete Kammer des Oberhauses (House of Lords) mit roten Ledersitzen und viel Gold und die schlichtere, überraschend kleine Kammer des Unterhauses (House of Commons). Das Wahrzeichen des Ensembles ist der 88 Meter hohe Uhrturm: Big Ben. Das Zifferblatt hat einen Durchmesser von acht Metern und vier Meter lange Zeiger.

Holmes: Da drüben wartet jemand auf uns, der mir viel besser gefällt als der Verräter Fawkes. Sie wissen, Watson, dass ich ein begeisterter Boxer bin. Aber ich würde mich davor hüten, gegen diesen Mann zu kämpfen. Das ist Ben Caunt.

Holmes zeigt auf eine hünenhafte Figur. Die eng sitzende Kniebundhose verrät, dass dieser Mann, passend zu seinem muskulösen Oberkörper, Oberschenkel wie Baumstämme besitzt. Das eckige Kinn schiebt er kampflustig nach vorn, aber unter der breiten Boxernase trägt er ein freundliches Lächeln.

Holmes: Ben, ich grüße Sie. Das ist Dr. Watson. Erzählen Sie ihm doch, wer Sie sind.
Ben Caunt: Ich war englischer Meister im Schwergewicht. Das ist lange her, aber ich bin sicher, dass, wer meine Kämpfe sah, mich nie vergaß. Mein letzter Kampf – ich war über 40 Jahre alt – ging über 60 Runden. Dann konnten wir

Then neither of us could stand up any more, and the referee called an end to it. When I was in my prime I could box for even longer – I once won in the 101st round.

Watson: And why have you come here, Mr Caunt, to Big Ben?

Ben Caunt: No secret about that. I AM Big Ben. The great bell in the tower, the one that chimes the hours, was named after me. After a while people started to use the name "Big Ben" for the whole tower. You look doubtful, but it's the truth. You probably heard that the bell got its name from Sir Benjamin Hall, a long-winded member of Parliament. He was a tall man, and he could speak in the House of Commons almost as long as I could fight. But when they inaugurated the bell, you could have asked anyone in London who Big Ben was, and nobody would have told you it was a politician.

Watson: Are you as big as the bell, then?

Ben Caunt: Not quite. It weighs 14 tons. You should have seen it, when a cart pulled by 16 horses carried it over the bridge. It took them 18 hours to haul it up into the bell chamber on ropes. They should have asked me for help.

Holmes: Ben, we have reason to believe that someone might be planning to damage the bell tower or the Houses of Parliament. We would be glad of your assistance.

Ben Caunt: Don't worry. Anyone who wants to attack Big Ben has to reckon with my fists. They won't get past me!

Holmes: Well, in that case I can report to the prime minister that there is no danger to the Houses of Parliament.

beide nicht mehr aufstehen, und der Ringrichter musste den Kampf abbrechen. Zu meinen besten Zeiten hielt ich sogar länger aus. Einmal gewann ich nach 101 Runden.

Watson: Und warum sind Sie hierhergekommen, Mr Caunt?

Ben Caunt: Das liegt doch auf der Hand. ICH bin Big Ben. Die große Glocke, die zur vollen Stunde schlägt, benannte man nach mir. Nach einiger Zeit fingen die Leute an, den Namen für den ganzen Turm «Big Ben» zu benutzen. Ja, Sie schauen skeptisch, aber so war es. Man hat Ihnen wohl erzählt, dass die Glocke nach Sir Benjamin Hall benannt wurde, diesem schwätzerischen Parlamentarier. Er war auch groß, und konnte fast so lange im House of Commons reden, wie ich kämpfte. Aber als die Glocke eingeweiht wurde, hätten Sie jeden Londoner fragen können, wer Big Ben ist. Keiner hätte Ihnen gesagt, dass es ein Politiker war.

Watson: Sind Sie denn so schwer wie die Glocke?

Ben Caunt: Nicht ganz! Die Glocke wiegt 14 Tonnen. Sie hätten sehen müssen, wie 16 Pferde sie über die Brücke zogen. Sie haben 18 Stunden gebraucht, um sie hoch in die Glockenkammer zu hieven. Sie hätten mich um Hilfe bitten sollen.

Holmes: Ben, wir haben den begründeten Verdacht, dass jemand einen Anschlag auf den Glockenturm oder die Houses of Parliament plant. Wir wären froh über Ihre Unterstützung.

Ben Caunt: Keine Sorge! Wer Big Ben zerstören will, muss mit meinen Fäusten rechnen. An mir kommt keiner vorbei!

Holmes: Dann kann ich dem Premierminister berichten, dass den Houses of Parliament keine Gefahr droht.

5.

A Famous Front Door
(No. 10 Downing Street)

Eine berühmte Haustür
(Downing Street Nr. 10)

We shape our buildings, and afterwards our
buildings shape us.

Winston Churchill

It is black, with a number 10 in white and a lion's
head for a knocker – and it is probably the world's
most famous front door. Innumerable prominent
people have been photographed in front of it. In
1931 Gandhi, spurning a suit even in the London
climate, appeared wrapped in his dhoti. Churchill liked to be seen here giving his V-for-victory
sign. To this day British prime ministers stand in the
street with the familiar door behind them to an-
nounce events such as their own resignations.
10 Downing Street has been the abode of prime
ministers since 1735. Its modest façade conceals
a warren of rooms: 100 of them on five floors, including elegant reception rooms, sober-looking
spaces for meetings, and many offices. The prime
minister's flat is on the third floor. There is a courtyard, a large house at the rear and, at the back of
it all, the rose garden and a terrace with a view
towards St James's Park.
This historic labyrinth of passages, rooms and stairs
has been remodelled repeatedly over three centuries and is considered, especially by the security
services, unfit to be the official seat of the leader of
a modern government, but the house has acquired
such symbolic importance that no prime minister
dares to move away. A thorough restoration took

Wir gestalten Gebäude, später formen sie uns.

Winston Churchill

Die wahrscheinlich berühmteste Haustür der Welt ist schwarz mit der Nummer 10 in Weiß und hat als Klopfer einen Löwenkopf. Zahllose Prominente wurden davor fotografiert, etwa Gandhi im Jahr 1931, der es trotz des Londoner Klimas ablehnte, einen Anzug zu tragen, und eingewickelt in seinem dhoti-Tuch erschien. Oder Churchill, der während des Zweiten Weltkriegs gern mit Victory-Zeichen grüßend dort erschien. Bis heute stehen britische Premierminister auf dieser Straße, mit der bekannten Tür im Rücken, um wichtige Neuigkeiten wie Rücktritte bekannt zu geben.

Downing Street Nr. 10 dient seit 1735 als Amtssitz des Premierministers. Hinter dem bescheidenen Eingang verbirgt sich ein Labyrinth von Zimmern: 100 an der Zahl auf fünf Etagen, darunter elegante Empfangs-säle, nüchterne Konferenzzimmer und viele Büros. Die Wohnung des Premierministers ist im dritten Ober-geschoss. Es gibt einen Innenhof, ein großes Hinter-haus und auf der Rückseite einen Rosengarten, Rasen-flächen und eine Terrasse mit Blick auf St James's Park. Dieses geschichtsträchtige Labyrinth aus Räumen und Treppen, seit 300 Jahren immer wieder umgestaltet, ist als Amtssitz eines Regierungschefs heute eigentlich ungeeignet, insbesondere aus Sicht des Sicherheits-diensts. Aber das Haus ist als Prestigesymbol so wichtig geworden, dass kein Premierminister es wagt, auszu-ziehen. In den 1960er-Jahren fand eine umfassende

place in the 1960s. This included inserting new foundations and cleaning the façade. When generations of soot had been removed from the walls, it was discovered that number ten was built of yellow brick, which was then painted black to preserve the familiar appearance. The original door, which has been replaced by a more secure installation, can be seen in the Churchill War Rooms (nearby in King Charles Street, daily 9.30 am – 6 pm).

Until the 1980s all passers-by had free access to Downing Street. Tourists could stroll past number 10 and take photos. However, fear of attack led Margaret Thatcher's government to install a guarded gate at the end of the short road, and the fears later proved to be justified: in 1991 the IRA fired mortars from a Ford Transit van that was parked close by in Whitehall. One of the projectiles made a deep crater in the garden and shattered window panes in the house. Today inquisitive visitors assemble on Whitehall and peer through the gates into Downing Street, but can glimpse little of what is going on beyond them.

Holmes and Watson give their names to the duty policeman and are admitted. A secretary takes Holmes to the prime minister and asks Watson to wait in the Cabinet Room. He takes a seat and looks at the long cabinet table, which is visible between two pairs of columns. Suddenly he notices that someone is standing next to him. The man has a curly wig, a long velvet coat with wide lapels and gilded buttons,

Sanierung statt. Diese beinhaltete neue Fundamente und eine Fassadenreinigung. Als die Mauern von jahrzehntealten Rußschichten befreit waren, stellte man fest, dass Nr. 10 aus gelben Ziegelsteinen gebaut worden war. Diese bekamen dann einen schwarzen Anstrich, um das gewohnte Bild zu bewahren. Die ursprüngliche Tür wurde durch eine Sicherheitstür ersetzt und ist in den Churchill War Rooms zu sehen (in der nahe gelegenen King Charles Street, täglich 9.30–18 Uhr).

Bis in die 1980er-Jahre hatte jeder freien Zugang zur Downing Street. Touristen konnten vorbeispazieren und Fotos machen. Aber aus Angst vor Attentaten ließ Margaret Thatchers Regierung am Ende der kurzen Straße ein Tor und Wachposten aufstellen. Die Angst erwies sich später als berechtigt: 1991 warf die Irisch-Republikanische Armee (IRA) Mörsergranaten von einem in der Straße Whitehall geparkten Ford Transit aus. Eines der Projektile hinterließ einen tiefen Krater im Garten und zerstörte Fensterscheiben. Heute versammeln sich neugierige Touristen auf der Straße Whitehall und spähen durch die Tore in die Downing Street, können aber wenig von dem sehen, was sich dort abspielt.

Holmes und Watson melden sich beim wachhabenden Polizisten und werden eingelassen. Ein Sekretär führt Holmes zum Büro des Premierministers und bittet Watson, im Cabinet Room zu warten. Er setzt sich und betrachtet den langen Tisch, der durch eine Öffnung zwischen zwei Säulenpaaren zu sehen ist. Auf einmal merkt er, dass jemand neben ihm steht. Der Mann trägt eine lockige Perücke, einen langen Samtrock mit breiten Aufschlägen und goldenen Knöpfen,

and beneath it a silk waistcoat decorated with a floral border in gold brocade.

Watson *(rises and gives an embarrassed cough)*: I hope I'm not disturbing anything. I was asked to wait here. My name is Dr John Watson. Your face seems familiar, but I'm afraid I can't recall your name.

Man in wig: My portrait is in the hall. I am Sir George Downing. I built this street.

Watson: Did you live here?

Sir George Downing: O no! That was quite out of the question. You see, I know how these houses were constructed, and took care to put a safe distance between London and myself by the time the work was finished. In 1675 I moved to Cambridge, and spent my retirement there in peace. The ground here is soft and water-logged, but of course I didn't want to fork out a fortune for the foundations, and that seems to have been the right decision. The old place is still standing.

Watson: How did you come to own the land?

Sir George Downing: King Charles II showed his gratitude to me for parting company with my old friends in the parliamentary party. I had been in charge of Oliver Cromwell's secret service, and had a lot of useful contacts. My skills as a diplomat were also highly valued, though I say it myself. When Cromwell died and the House of Stuart was restored to the throne, I could see which way the wind was blowing, and it seemed opportune to adapt to the new circumstances – which I did, and that brought its rewards. The land that His Majesty granted to me was prime property even in those days.

darunter eine seidene Weste mit einer geblümten Borte aus
Goldbrokat.

Watson *(erhebt sich und hustet verlegen)*: Ich hoffe, ich
störe nicht. Man bat mich, hier zu warten. Mein Name ist
Dr. John Watson. Ihr Gesicht kommt mir bekannt vor, aber
ich fürchte, Ihres Namens kann ich mich nicht entsinnen.

Mann mit Perücke: In der Eingangshalle hängt mein Porträt.
Ich heiße Sir George Downing. Ich baute diese Straße.

Watson: Haben Sie hier gewohnt?

Sir George Downing: O nein! Das kam nicht infrage. Ich
weiß nämlich, wie diese Häuser gebaut sind, wenn Sie verstehen, was ich meine, und achtete darauf, dass ich in siche-
rer Entfernung von London war, als sie fertig wurden – im
Jahre 1675 zog ich nach Cambridge und verbrachte dort in
Frieden meinen Lebensabend. Der Boden hier ist weich und
feucht. Ich wollte natürlich kein Vermögen für Fundamente
ausgeben, und das scheint die richtige Entscheidung gewesen zu sein. Das alte Gebäude steht schließlich noch.

Watson: Wie kamen Sie in den Besitz der Grundstücke?

Sir George Downing: König Charles II. zeigte sich erkenntlich, weil ich mich von meinen ehemaligen Freunden der
parlamentarischen Partei trennte. Ich hatte Oliver Crom-
wells Geheimdienst geleitet und hatte viele nützliche Kon-
takte. Man schätzte auch meine Fähigkeiten als Diplomat
sehr, wenn ich das so sagen darf. Als Cromwell starb und
das Haus Stuart wieder an die Macht gebracht wurde,
wusste ich, wie der Hase läuft. Es schien sinnvoll, sich mit
den neuen Verhältnissen abzufinden – was ich tat, und das
wurde belohnt. Das Land, das mir seine Majestät schenkte,
war schon damals ein wahres Filetstück, ganz in der Nähe

It was close to Whitehall Palace, the royal residence in my time, and just a stone's throw from St James's Park. I put 15 houses on the site and sold them all in two shakes of a lamb's tail to persons of standing in society. A thoroughly satisfactory piece of business!

Watson: And one of those persons was the prime minister, I suppose. Congratulations!

Sir George Downing: No, no, that didn't happen until 50 years later. Walpole was the man's name, the king's chief minister, the one they describe as the first prime minister. There he is, above the fireplace – the artist rendered his cunning features extremely well. He had three houses converted to make this single big one. Sir Robert Walpole – what a scoundrel he was! People say that I was astute and knew how to look after number one, but you can't imagine how much treasure Walpole put aside for himself and his family over 20 years in office. I take my hat off to him. He became so rich that he could propose to the king that this house should be made available to all his successors in the office, rather than keeping it for himself personally. And that's the way it has remained, right up till now. By the way, he had a first-class architect called William Kent. I was amazed when I saw how beautifully the rooms of my old houses had been decorated.

Watson: I was told that cabinet meetings are held in this room.

Sir George Downing: That's right. I keep an eye on them. They need a long table to find space for all those unnecessary ministers. The prime minister sits on that chair in the middle, not at the end – it's the only one with armrests.

vom Whitehall Palace – zu meiner Zeit die königliche Residenz– und nur ein Katzensprung vom St James's Park. Ich baute 15 Häuser und verkaufte sie alle im Handumdrehen an Leute aus der feinen Gesellschaft. Ein wirklich wunderbares Geschäft!

Watson: Und unter den feinen Leuten war vermutlich der Premierminister. Glückwunsch!

Sir George Downing: Nein, das kam erst 50 Jahre später. Walpole hieß er, königlicher Ministerpräsident, der Mann, den man den ersten Premierminister nennt. Da ist er, über dem Kamin – der Künstler hat seine verschmitzten Gesichtszüge extrem gut getroffen. Er ließ drei Häuser zu diesem einen Großen umbauen. Sir Robert Walpole – was für ein Ganove! Man sagt mir nach, ich sei schlau und listig und auf meinen eigenen Vorteil bedacht gewesen, aber Sie können sich gar nicht vorstellen, wie viel Walpole in 20 Jahren Amtszeit für sich und seine Familie beiseitegeschafft hat, da kann ich nur sagen: Hut ab! Er wurde so reich, er konnte dem König vorschlagen, dass dieses Haus nicht ihm persönlich, sondern seinen Amtsnachfolgern zur Verfügung gestellt wird. So blieb es auch, bis heute. Er hatte übrigens einen sehr guten Architekten, William Kent. Ich staunte, als ich sah, wie schön die Interieurs in meinen Häusern gestaltet wurden.

Watson: In diesem Raum finden Kabinettssitzungen statt, sagte man mir gerade.

Sir George Downing: Richtig. Ich wohne ihnen immer bei. Sie brauchen einen langen Tisch, damit die ganzen überflüssigen Minister Platz finden. Der Premierminister sitzt auf dem Stuhl mittig am Tisch, nicht am Ende, es ist der einzige Stuhl mit Armlehnen.

Watson: To think of all the great men who once sat here! The statesmen who stood up to Napoleon – William Pitt the Younger, and the Duke of Wellington.

Sir George Downing: Wellington was a man you could respect. He had style. But Pitt? He was prime minister at the age of 24, the fool, instead of misspending his youth the way you're supposed to. He held office for 20 years, worked himself to death and bequeathed nothing but debts. Now tell me, how is it possible to hold power so long, have everything in the palm of your hand, and then die a poor man?

Watson: You may scoff, Sir George, but your street is a noble place, and it lifts the spirits to be here.

Sir George Downing: If only you knew! Before it came into my hands, the site was called the Cockpit, because cockfights took place here. Later its closeness to the park was the attraction for some residents, because that's where ladies of easy virtue waited for customers. Back in those days there were taverns in the street, not just the dull government offices that you see now. And I doubt whether what happens at this address today really is morally better than in the days of the Cockpit. The goings-on at this table can be as cruel as a cockfight, and the stakes are higher. Well, it's time for me to go. The present occupant of the house is arriving.

The prime minister, Lord Salisbury, and Holmes enter the Cabinet Room.

Lord Salisbury: Dr Watson, your vigorous support for Mr Holmes is well known. The city of London, indeed the kingdom, is facing a serious threat. I

Watson: Wenn ich daran denke, wer alles hier war! Die großen Staatsmänner, die Napoleon die Stirn boten – William Pitt der Jüngere, später der Duke von Wellington.

Sir George Downing: Wellington war ein ehrenwerter Mann, er hatte Stil. Aber Pitt? Premierminister mit 24 Jahren, was für ein Idiot! Statt seine Jugend zu genießen, wie man es sollte. 20 Jahre blieb er im Amt, hat sich zu Tode gearbeitet und hinterließ nichts als Schulden. Sagen Sie mir, wie ist es möglich, dass man so lange an den Hebeln der Macht sitzt und dann hoch verschuldet stirbt?

Watson: Sie spotten, aber Ihre Straße ist ein erhabener Ort, Sir George, und hier zu sein hebt meine Stimmung.

Sir George Downing: Wenn Sie nur wüssten! Bevor sie in meine Hände fiel, wurde die Gegend Cockpit (dt. Hahnenkampfplatz) genannt, weil hier Hahnenkämpfe stattfanden. Später gefiel manch einem die Adresse wegen der Nähe zum Park, weil dort leichte Mädchen auf ihre Freier warteten. Es gab damals auch Kneipen in der Straße, nicht nur langweilige Ämter, die Sie hier sehen. Und ich habe meine Zweifel, ob das, was heute hier passiert, wirklich anständiger ist als derzeit in Cockpit. Was an diesem Tisch passiert, kann so grausam wie Hahnenkämpfe sein, nur die Einsätze sind höher. Es ist Zeit, dass ich verschwinde, der derzeitige Amtsinhaber kommt.

Der Premierminister, Lord Salisbury, und Holmes betreten gemeinsam den Cabinet Room.

Lord Salisbury: Mr Watson, bekanntlich leisten Sie Mr Holmes tatkräftige Unterstützung. Die Stadt London, ja sogar das ganze Königreich, ist einer schlimmen Bedrohung

rely on you both to ward off the danger. As you are aware, it is only seven days since I became prime minister again, and I don't want my new term of office to begin with a disaster. Now God be with you!

Holmes and Watson leave Downing Street and turn left into Whitehall.

Holmes: Lord Salisbury has received an anonymous letter. I would say it was written by an impulsive man of great self-confidence, who keeps his cards close to his chest. He threatens an attack that will cause ruinous costs and damage the reputation of the government – unless he receives one million pounds. Details of a hand-over are to be given later this evening. The writing paper is of a common kind. The envelope and the postmark reveal nothing of importance. Now Watson, do you remember the dreadful railway accident that took place in Acton last year? It was, in truth, no accident. Lord Salisbury's predecessor received a similar blackmail letter, but did not think it was genuine until the tragedy happened. The whole thing was hushed up. I suspected as much at the time, but no-one had the wisdom to call for my help. Lord Salisbury has informed Scotland Yard, but he does not believe that the police can solve the case in time to prevent a disaster. We have a busy day ahead of us, Watson!

ausgesetzt. Ich verlasse mich darauf, dass Sie beide die Gefahr abwenden. Ich bin, wie Sie sicher wissen, erst seit sieben Tagen wieder Premierminister und möchte nicht, dass meine neue Amtszeit mit einer Katastrophe beginnt. Gott sei mit Ihnen!

Holmes und Watson verlassen Downing Street und biegen links in die Whitehall ab.

Holmes: Lord Salisbury hat ein anonymes Schreiben erhalten. Der Handschrift nach zu urteilen, wurde es von einem impulsiven Mann mit ausgeprägtem Selbstbewusstsein verfasst, jemandem, der nicht gerne etwas preisgibt. Er droht, einen Anschlag mit schwerwiegenden wirtschaftlichen Folgen und Verlust an Ansehen für die Regierung zu verüben – es sei denn, die Summe von einer Million Pfund wird übergeben. Die Einzelheiten zur Übergabe werden später mitgeteilt. Das Schreibpapier ist überall erhältlich. Das Kuvert und der Poststempel verraten auch nichts von Bedeutung. Watson, Sie erinnern sich an das schreckliche Eisenbahnunglück in Acton letztes Jahr? Das war in Wahrheit kein Unfall. Lord Salisburys Vorgänger erhielt einen ähnlichen Drohbrief, den man nicht ernst nahm, bis es zur Tragödie kam. Die ganze Sache wurde vertuscht. Ich ahnte es schon damals, aber leider hatte keiner die Geistesgegenwärtigkeit, mich zurate zu ziehen. Lord Salisbury hat Scotland Yard verständigt, zweifelt aber, dass die Polizei den Fall rechtzeitig lösen und eine Katastrophe verhindern kann. Wir haben heute viel zu tun, Watson!

6.

The King and his Painter
(The Banqueting House)

Der König und der Malerfürst
(Banqueting House)

Uneasy lies the head that wears a crown.

From *Henry IV*, Part II, William Shakespeare

> The Banqueting House is the only surviving part of the enormous, rambling Whitehall Palace, one of the Tudor and Stuart monarchs' main residences. After almost the entire palace burned down in 1698, the Banqueting House was used as a chapel and concert hall until 1890, then as a military museum. Today, following restoration, it is one of a group of royal properties that admits visitors (www.hrp.org.uk, Mon - Sat 10 am - 5 pm).

From Downing Street Holmes and Watson walk a little way along Whitehall, cross the street and stop in front of an imposing two-storey building that is crowned by a stone balustrade.

Holmes: The Banqueting House is a historic building and a symbol of government authority. This could make it the target of an attack. I will examine it thoroughly from the outside. Go inside, Watson, and have a look around.

Watson walks down a few steps to the lower floor, where a wide staircase leads him upwards again to a large room that has the full height of two storeys. Huge paintings adorn the ceiling, from which magnificent chandeliers are suspended.

Watson: What a grisly sight! A headless man! Could this be King Charles I?

Schwer ruht das Haupt, das eine Krone drückt!

Aus ‹Heinrich IV.›, William Shakespeare

> Das Banqueting House ist der einzige verbleibende
> Teil des riesigen Whitehall Palace, eine der Haupt-
> residenzen der Tudor- und Stuart-Monarchen.
> Nachdem beinahe der ganze Palast 1698 abbrannte,
> wurde das Banqueting House bis 1890 als Kapelle und
> Konzertsaal genutzt, dann als Militärmuseum. Heute –
> nach der Restaurierung – gehört es zu einer Gruppe
> königlicher Paläste, die ihre Pforten für Besucher
> öffnen (www.hrp.org.uk, Mo-Sa 10-15 Uhr).

Von der Downing Street gehen Holmes und Watson eine
Weile Whitehall entlang, überqueren die Straße und machen
halt vor einem imposanten zweistöckigen Bauwerk, das ein
steinernes Geländer krönt.

Holmes: Das Banqueting House ist ein bedeutendes histori-
sches Gebäude und ein Symbol der Regierungsmacht, also
ein exponiertes Ziel für einen Anschlag. Ich werde es von
außen gründlich untersuchen. Gehen Sie hinein, Watson,
und schauen Sie sich um.

Watson steigt einige Stufen in das untere Geschoss hinab.
Dort führt eine breite Treppe wieder nach oben. Er betritt
einen hohen Saal, der sich über beide Obergeschosse erstreckt. Großflächige Malereien schmücken die Decke, von
der prächtige Leuchter hängen.

Watson: Oh, was ein schauderhafter Anblick! Ein Mensch
ohne Kopf. Ist das vielleicht König Charles I.?

A strange apparition approaches him. The figure is sumptuously dressed in a coat of glistening brown silk, and has a spreading collar of delicate lace to cover its shoulders – but there is indeed no head on the shoulders. Instead the figure is holding a head beneath its right arm. Watson observes that the head has a well-groomed pointed beard and long, dark hair, parted at the centre. He steps back in fright when the mouth opens and speaks to him.

Charles I: Calm yourself, there is nothing to fear. I am pleased to have a visitor to my Banqueting House. Do you know what happened to me here? My own subjects beheaded me! Right here, on a scaffold in front of the finest building in my own royal palace grounds. Stay a while, and I'll tell you the whole story.

Watson: Your Majesty, I would be honoured to hear it from your own lips. Perhaps you would be so gracious as to remind me when these horrible events took place?

Charles I: Well, every schoolboy knows that! It was the year of our Lord 1649, of course. The Parliamentarians had defeated my army. I was betrayed and handed over to my enemies. They put me on trial in Westminster Hall. I need not say that I refused to recognise the authority of the court. I was the ruler of England and Scotland by divine right, and no parliament could pass judgement over me. Nevertheless, the false wretches condemned me to death as a traitor and murderer. I spent my last night in the old palace on the other side of St James's Park, and said farewell to my children there. Then an armed escort brought me here – on

Eine seltsame Erscheinung kommt auf ihn zu. Sie ist kostbar gekleidet in eine Jacke aus glänzender brauner Seide. Ein breiter Kragen aus feinster Spitze bedeckt die Schultern – aber auf diesen Schultern befindet sich tatsächlich kein Kopf. Stattdessen hält die Figur den Kopf unter dem rechten Arm. Watson sieht einen gepflegten Spitzbart und lange dunkle Haare mit Mittelscheitel. Er schreckt zurück, als der Mund sich öffnet und ihn anspricht.

Charles I.: Ruhig Blut, fürchten Sie sich nicht! Ich freue mich, dass mich jemand in meinem Bankettpalast besucht. Wissen Sie, was mir hier zugestoßen ist? Meine eigenen Untertanen haben mich enthauptet! Direkt hier, auf einem Schafott vor dem schönsten Gebäude auf meinen Palastgelände. Bleiben Sie eine Weile, und ich erzähle Ihnen die ganze Geschichte.

Watson: Majestät, es wäre eine Ehre, die Geschichte aus Ihrem eigenen Mund zu hören. Würden Sie mich bitte daran erinnern, wann sich dieses furchtbare Ereignis zugetragen hat?

Charles I.: Das weiß doch jedes Kind! Im Jahre des Herrn 1649 natürlich. Die Parlamentarier hatten meine Armeen besiegt, ich wurde verraten und an meine Feinde übergeben. Sie machten mir den Prozess in der Westminster Hall. Ich erkannte das Gericht natürlich nicht an – ich war Monarch von England und Schottland durch Gottes Gnaden, kein Parlament hatte Autorität über mich. Aber sie verurteilten mich trotzdem als Verräter und Mörder. Meine letzte Nacht verbrachte ich im alten Palast auf der anderen Seite von St James's Park, wo ich mich von meinen Kindern verabschiedete. Dann wurde ich von einem bewaffneten Geleit zu Fuß hierhin gebracht – ich, der Kö-

foot. I, the king, was not allowed to ride. What a humiliation! I had to pass through this window to a scaffold that they had erected in front of the hall. I am proud of how I conducted myself. It was a cold day, so I put on two shirts to make sure I did not shiver. That would have given the impression that I was afraid. I declared to the assembled crowd that the Almighty was on my side. And so it proved to be. Eleven years later a king from the House of Stuart once more ascended the throne: that was my son Charles.

Watson: May I ask why you are here, if the place holds such bad memories?

Charles I: This great room demonstrates the glories of the House of Stuart. My father, King James I, commissioned Inigo Jones, the best architect in the land, to build it. Jones had travelled to Italy and brought back a completely new style of architecture. This Banqueting House was a sensation. There was nothing comparable to it in all England. When my father died, I commemorated him here. The paintings on the ceiling are a representation of his just and wise rule. Yes, that's my contribution – these wonderful paintings.

Watson: Who was the artist?

Charles I: Rubens, that was his name. He was from Flanders. He first came to London as a diplomat, as an ambassador from the King of Spain. I knighted him: Sir Peter Paul Rubens. He was a proud man, not like our English painters, who were no better than humble craftsmen. He was a man of standing, wealthy and educated, and he was acquainted with life at a royal court. Everyone said he was the best painter far and wide,

nig, durfte nicht reiten, so eine Erniedrigung! Schließlich musste ich aus dem Fenster steigen zu einem Schafott, das sie vor der Halle errichtet hatten. Ich bin stolz darauf, wie würdevoll ich mich verhalten habe. Ich zog ein zweites Hemd an – der Tag war eisig, ich wollte nicht vor Kälte zittern und den Eindruck erwecken, ängstlich zu sein – und erklärte den Anwesenden, dass der Allmächtige auf meiner Seite stehe. Und so war es auch. Elf Jahre später saß wieder ein König aus dem Hause Stuart auf dem Thron: mein Sohn Charles.

Watson: Darf ich fragen, warum Sie sich hier aufhalten, wenn dieser Ort doch so schlimme Erinnerungen birgt?

Charles I.: Dieser Bankettsaal zeigt, wie glorreich das Hause Stuart regierte. Mein Vater, James I., hat ihn bauen lassen – von Inigo Jones, dem besten Architekten des Königreichs. Jones reiste durch Italien und brachte einen völlig neuen Architekturstil nach England. Dieses Bauwerk war eine Sensation, es gab nichts Vergleichbares im ganzen Lande. Als mein Vater starb, habe ich ihm hier ein Denkmal gesetzt. Die Deckengemälde stellen seine weise und gerechte Herrschaft dar. Ja, diese herrlichen Malereien sind mein Beitrag.

Watson: Wer war der Maler?

Charles I.: Rubens, so war sein Name. Er stammte aus Flandern und kam als Diplomat nach London, als Gesandter des spanischen Königs. Ich adelte ihn damals: Sir Peter Paul Rubens. Er hielt viel auf sich, benahm sich nicht wie unsere englischen Maler, die nur bessere Handwerker waren. Er war ein angesehener Mann, wohlhabend und gebildet, und gewöhnt an ein fürstliches Leben am Hof. Alle sagten, er sei der beste Maler des Kontinents, und so

so how could I employ anyone else to do the work? But the costs were monstrous. 3,000 pounds! And this Rubens, with his airs as a gentleman, didn't work lying on his back under my ceiling. Oh no, that was much too uncomfortable for him. All the paintings were done on canvas in his studio in Antwerp, then rolled up for transport, and attached to frames in the ceiling here. It was worth all the trouble, no doubt about that. Look at the large oval in the centre. That's the apotheosis of my father. Yes, it's called an apotheosis – it means he's ascending to heaven, surrounded by gods and goddesses.

Watson: Magnificent! The paintings truly set the scene for royal festivities! I wish I could have been present at your celebrations.

Charles I: Well, unfortunately there were difficulties about that. As the paintings were so valuable, we couldn't expose them to the soot rising from candles. That was the end of all the great festivities – at least here, in the Banqueting House. Before Rubens did his work, we used to have the most wonderful entertainments in this room: masques, with music, dancing and verse. Afterwards, I used the place to receive ambassadors. As you see, it makes a fine impression, and a bit of ostentation is just what you need when dealing with foreign powers. Have you noticed that this hall has the shape of a double cube? It's as tall as it is wide, but twice as long. The architect said those are the perfect proportions.

Watson: Your Majesty, it is possible that someone is planning an outrage against this fine building. Have you seen anything unusual here, such as people with explosives?

konnte ich natürlich keinen anderen nehmen. Aber die Kosten! 3000 Pfund! Rubens mit seinem vornehmen Getue arbeitete auch nicht vor Ort auf dem Rücken liegend. Nein, das war ihm zu unbequem. Alles wurde auf Leinwand in seinem Atelier in Antwerpen gemalt, für den Transport zusammengerollt und dann hier in den Rahmen an der Decke angebracht. Es hat sich aber zweifellos gelohnt. Schauen Sie mal auf das große Oval in der Mitte: Das zeigt die Apotheose meines Vaters. Ja, das nennt man eine Apotheose – es bedeutet, dass er in den Himmel steigt, von Göttern und Göttinnen begleitet.

Watson: Großartig! Was für eine Kulisse für königliche Feierlichkeiten! Ich hätte Ihre Feste hier gerne miterlebt.

Charles I.: Tja, leider gestaltete es sich schwierig. Weil die Gemälde so kostbar sind, konnten wir sie dem Kerzenruß nicht aussetzen, und die Feste mussten aufhören – zumindest im Banqueting House. Bevor Rubens sein Werk fertigstellte, hatten wir die wunderbarste Unterhaltung in diesem Saal: Maskenspiele mit Musik, Tanz, Dichtung. Nachher nutzte ich den Saal, um Botschafter zu empfangen: Dieser Raum macht Eindruck! Und ein bisschen Prahlerei gegenüber ausländischen Mächten ist nie verkehrt. Ist Ihnen schon aufgefallen, dass dieser Raum die Form eines Doppelkubus hat? Die gleiche Höhe und Breite, aber doppelt so lang. Die vollkommenen Proportionen, meinte der Architekt.

Watson: Eure Majestät, es gibt Hinweise, dass jemand einen Anschlag auf dieses Haus verüben möchte. Haben Sie hier etwas Ungewöhnliches gesehen, Menschen mit Sprengstoff vielleicht?

Charles I: I pay very close attention to what goes on in my Banqueting House. You may depend upon it. Yesterday a dark-looking person was loitering at the back of the building, trying to force open the windows. I gave him the fright of his life. I don't believe he'll be back in a hurry. And it's time that you left, too. Your audience with the king is over. But remember this: we of the royal House of Stuart are the rightful kings according to God's will. It is wise to show us respect. A Charles or a James may be sitting on the throne again sooner than you expect.

Watson bows to take his leave, and descends the staircase to the street. At that very moment Sherlock Holmes appears from around the corner of the building.

Holmes: I see you are rubbing your neck, Watson, and there's a crease in your collar. Were you impressed by the ceiling paintings? While you were looking at pictures, I was examining the windows, and I found some suspicious-looking scratches on the frames. They were made by this iron bar, which was lying on the ground. Somebody wanted to break in, but was forced to leave in a hurry.

Watson: Yes, I know.

Holmes *(gives Watson a keen look)*: Another ghost protecting the place? In that case we don't need to ask Scotland Yard to put a guard on the building. We'll go straight to Trafalgar Square. Mays said that was his passenger's next stop.

As they walk up Whitehall towards Trafalgar Square, Holmes and Watson pass the street called Great

Charles I.: Ich achte sehr genau darauf, was im Banqueting House vor sich geht, das können Sie mir glauben. Gestern lauerte eine dunkle Gestalt an der Rückseite des Hauses und versuchte, die Fenster aufzustemmen. Ich habe ihm den Schreck seines Lebens eingejagt, so schnell wird er, glaube ich, nicht noch mal auftauchen. Es ist Zeit, dass auch Sie gehen! Die Audienz mit dem König ist vorbei. Und vergessen Sie nicht: Wir aus dem Hause Stuart sind die von Gott erwählten Herrscher. Zollen Sie uns besser Respekt, denn vielleicht sitzt bald wieder ein Charles oder James auf dem Thron.

Watson verneigt sich zum Abschied vor dem König und nimmt die Treppe zur Straße hinunter. Im selben Augenblick kommt Sherlock Holmes um die Ecke.

Holmes: Ich sehe, Sie reiben sich den Nacken, Watson, und Sie haben einen Knick im Kragen. Gefielen Ihnen die Deckenmalereien? Während Sie sich die Bilder anschauten, habe ich an den Fensterrahmen hinten verdächtige Kratzer entdeckt. Sie stammen von einer Brechstange, die am Boden lag – dort wollte jemand einbrechen, ist aber offensichtlich in Eile abgezogen.

Watson: Das stimmt, ich weiß es schon.

Holmes *(schaut Watson prüfend an)***:** Wieder ein Geist, der diesen Ort beschützt? Dann müssen wir Scotland Yard nicht bitten, das Gebäude zu überwachen. Wir gehen jetzt zum Trafalgar Square. Das war, sagte Mays, die nächste Station von seinem Fahrgast.

Auf dem Weg entlang Whitehall in Richtung Trafalgar Square passieren Holmes und Watson auf der rechten

Scotland Yard on the right-hand side. The likely origin of the name is that Scottish ambassadors to the English court were based here in the Middle Ages. After the founding of the Metropolitan Police in 1829, the first "Bobbies", so called because "Robert" was the first name of Prime Minister Peel, worked in the adjacent Whitehall Place, and later occupied numbers 8 and 9. In 1890 the police force moved to New Scotland Yard on the banks of the Thames, and is now based on Broadway, near St James's Park tube station.

Seite die Straße Great Scotland Yard. Der Ursprung des Namens liegt wahrscheinlich in der Repräsentanz des schottischen Königreichs am englischen Hof im Mittelalter. Nach Gründung der Metropolitan Police 1829 arbeiteten die ersten «Bobbies» – so genannt, weil der damalige Premierminister Peel den Vornamen «Robert» hatte – im benachbarten Whitehall Place und besetzten später auch die Hausnummern 8 und 9 in Great Scotland Yard. 1890 zog die Polizei in eigens gebaute Räumlichkeiten am Themseufer um, die den Namen New Scotland Yard erhielten. Heute befindet sich das Hauptquartier der Londoner Polizei an der Straße Broadway nahe dem U-Bahnhof St James's Park.

7.

A National Hero
(Trafalgar Square)

Ein Volksheld
(Trafalgar Square)

England expects that every man will do his duty.

Nelson's signal to his fleet
at the Battle of Trafalgar

Trafalgar Square is the geographical centre of London. The south side of the square, where an equestrian statue of Charles I now stands, was the site of the old Charing Cross, one of a series of crosses erected by Edward I in memory of his wife Eleanor of Castile. It was midway between the two settlements from which modern London emerged: to the west was Westminster, the royal quarter and seat of government, while to the east lay the City of London, a centre of trade since Roman times. The distances between London and other places in Britain are traditionally measured from the site of the original Charing Cross. The tall stone cross that now stands in front of Charing Cross railway station, 50 metres to the east, was built in 1865. In 1829 the architect John Nash demolished a maze of alleys and buildings. At its northern end, the area once occupied by the stables of the Royal Mews, the National Gallery now stands, at the north-eastern corner the Church of St Martin-in-the-Fields. Stone plinths on the square bear statues of King George IV and two empire-builders who made their names in India, Henry Havelock and Charles Napier. The north-western plinth remained empty and is now famous as the "fourth plinth", which provides a space for new, often controversial, forms of artistic expression.

England erwartet, dass jedermann seine Pflicht tut.

Signal von Admiral Nelson an seine Flotte
bei der Schlacht von Trafalgar

Trafalgar Square ist der geografische Mittelpunkt von London: An seiner Südseite, wo heute ein Reiterdenkmal von Charles I. steht, war einst das alte Hochkreuz, Charing Cross. Es war eines von vielen, die Edward I. in Gedenken an seine Frau Eleanor of Castile errichten ließ. Das Kreuz stand auf halber Strecke zwischen den beiden Siedlungen, aus denen das moderne London entstand: Im Westen lag das Königs- und Regierungsviertel Westminster, östlich die City of London, die seit römischer Zeit ein Handelszentrum war. Traditionell werden die Entfernungen von London zu anderen Orten in Großbritannien vom ursprünglichen Standpunkt des Charing Cross aus bemessen. 1865 wurde das große Steinkreuz erbaut, das heute vor dem Bahnhof Charing Cross, 50 Meter weiter östlich, steht, 1829 riss der Architekt John Nash ein Wirrwarr kleiner Gassen und Häuser ab, um einen öffentlichen Platz zu schaffen. An der Nordseite des Platzes, früher Standort der königlichen Stallungen, steht jetzt die National Gallery, an der Nordostecke die Kirche St Martin-in-the-Fields. Steinsockel auf dem Platz tragen Statuen von König George IV. und zwei Männern, Henry Havelock und Charles Napier, die die britische Herrschaft in Indien ausbauten. Der nordwestliche Steinsockel blieb leer und ist heute als «vierter Sockel» bekannt, der einen Ausstellungsort für neue, oft kontroverse Kunstwerke bietet.

Two large fountain basins and four bronze lions frame Nelson's Column, which has been crowned since 1843 by a statue of the naval hero Lord Horatio Nelson. On October 5th, 1805, at Cape Trafalgar off the Spanish coast, Nelson annihilated the French and Spanish fleets. Though he lost his own life in the battle, his victory ended the danger of invasion by Napoleon's armies and secured the supremacy of British sea power.

Holmes and Watson walk north along Whitehall to reach Trafalgar Square. They cross the road to the centre of the square and look at the bronze reliefs that depict Nelson's naval victories at the base of the column.

Holmes: If an enemy of the state plots to destroy a symbol of the Empire, Nelson's Column might well be his first target. I wonder who could advise us here.

As he speaks, a powerfully built man watches him from the side. The man is wearing the clothing of a building worker: a blue shirt of tough weave, a red neckerchief and thick black trousers worn shiny by heavy use.

Building worker: If you're looking for someone who knows Nelson's Column, then I'm your man. Daniel Briggs is the name. I was the foreman on site when we put up the column, and I supervised the work when we placed the admiral on top.

Holmes: We would be interested to know how a wrongdoer might be able to damage the column. Does it have any weak points?

Zwei große Brunnen und vier bronzene Löwen umgeben Nelson's Column, seit 1843 eine mit der Statue des hochverehrten Marinehelden Lord Horatio Nelson gekrönte Säule. Am 5. Oktober 1805 besiegte Nelson die französisch-spanische Flotte vor der spanischen Küste bei Kap Trafalgar, verlor aber während der Schlacht sein Leben. Der Sieg bannte die Gefahr einer Invasion durch Napoleons Armeen und sicherte die weltweite Überlegenheit der britischen Seemacht.

Vom nördlichen Ende der Whitehall erreichen Holmes und Watson Trafalgar Square. Sie überqueren die Straße zur Platzmitte und betrachten die Bronzereliefs am Fuß der Säule, die Nelsons Seeschlachten darstellen.

Holmes: Wenn ein Staatsfeind ein Symbol des Empire zerstören will, dann steht Nelson's Column ganz oben auf der Liste möglicher Ziele. Wer uns wohl hier weiterhelfen könnte?

Während er spricht, beobachtet ein kräftig gebauter Mann ihn von der Seite. Er trägt die Kleidung eines Bauarbeiters: ein blaues Hemd aus festem Stoff, ein rotes Halstuch und eine abgewetzte schwarze Hose.

Bauarbeiter: Wenn Sie jemand suchen, der sich mit der Nelson's Column auskennt, dann sind Sie bei mir richtig. Daniel Briggs ist mein Name. Ich war der Polier, als wir die Säule errichtet haben. Ich habe die Bauarbeiten überwacht, als wir den Admiral oben aufgestellt haben.

Holmes: Uns interessiert die Frage, wie ein Übeltäter die Säule beschädigen könnte. Besitzt sie irgendwelche Schwachstellen?

Daniel Briggs: Certainly not! Are you suggesting we didn't do the work properly? Take a good look, and rub your hand over the stone. That's Dartmoor granite, right to the top of the column, all 150 feet of it. You won't find a more durable stone anywhere. The column is almost 12 feet across, so it's extremely stable. We used the latest methods to construct it. We even had a steam engine on wheels to lift the stones to the top – the heaviest of them weighed ten tons, and that's a strain if you only have muscle power. The scaffolding construction was the cleverest thing you ever saw, and folk from the building trade came from far and wide to study it. And when the column was finished, before we hoisted up the statue of the admiral, what do you think we did, the stonemasons and me? We ate a dinner fit for a king on the platform at the top, all 14 of us round one table. That's how big the column is. And we drank to Lord Nelson. No-one ever deserved a toast from honest working men more than he did.

Watson: He was truly a man of great stature!

Daniel Briggs: 18 feet tall he is – that's the statue, of course. They say he wasn't a big man in life, but he was certainly a hero. The sculptors who did these scenes in bronze on the base told me what they show. This one's the Battle of St Vincent. Nelson ignored orders, sailed his ship out of the line, and attacked three Spanish men o' war all at once.

Holmes: And this side of the column depicts a famous story. That must be the Battle of Copenhagen, where he disobeyed orders again – or rather, he held his telescope to his blind eye so that he couldn't see

Daniel Briggs: Nein, ganz sicher nicht! Meinen Sie etwa, wir hätten schlampig gearbeitet? Sehen Sie genau hin und fühlen Sie mal den Stein – Granit aus dem Dartmoor von unten bis oben, alle 150 Fuß (= 46 Meter). Einen beständigeren Stein finden Sie nirgendwo, und mit einer Breite von fast 12 Fuß (= 3,5 Meter) ist die Säule sehr stabil. Außerdem arbeiteten wir nach den neuesten Methoden. Wir hatten sogar eine Dampfmaschine auf Rädern, um die Steine an die Spitze zu heben – bis zu zehn Tonnen wogen sie, und das ist zu schwer, wenn Sie nur Muskelkraft zur Verfügung haben. Das Gerüst war die schlaueste Konstruktion überhaupt, und Leute aus dem Baugewerbe kamen von nah und fern, um es sich anzusehen. Und was glauben Sie, was die Steinmetze und ich machten, als die Säule fertig und die Statue noch nicht drauf war? Wir speisten wie die Könige dort oben, Roastbeef und Ale für 14 Mann, alle an einem großen Tisch. So viel Platz ist dort. Wir tranken auf Lord Nelson. Kein anderer hat es je so verdient, dass ehrlich arbeitende Leute auf ihn anstoßen!

Watson: Wahrlich ein großer Mann!

Daniel Briggs: 18 Fuß (= 5,5 Meter) groß ist er – natürlich als Statue. Im Leben war er klein, sagt man, aber er war in jeder Hinsicht ein echter Held. Die Bildhauer erzählten mir, was sie auf den Bronzeplatten am Sockel darstellten. Hier ist die Schlacht von St. Vincent. Nelson ignorierte Befehle, segelte aus der Reihe und griff gleich drei spanische Kriegsschiffe mit seinem eigenen an.

Holmes: Und diese Seite der Säule zeigt eine berühmte Geschichte. Das ist wohl die Schlacht von Kopenhagen, wo er wieder einen Befehl missachtete oder, genauer gesagt, sein Teleskop an das blinde Auge hielt, damit er das Signal zum

the signal to retreat. Nelson was a vigorous man of action, a man with a mind of his own.

Daniel Briggs: He never let the powers that be tell him what to do. And that's an example to us all. Now look at this side of the column. It's a scene from the Battle of the Nile. They brought him into the cabin with a head wound. The surgeon turned away from the sailor he was treating, and came over to the admiral straight away, but what did Nelson say? "I'll wait with my brave comrades until it's my turn." He had lost his right arm and he was blind in one eye, but he always exposed himself in the thick of battle. I was proud to work on his monument. And the people love him, even though the lords and gentlemen who decided to honour Lord Nelson on this square had no love of the people.

Watson: What do you mean by that?

Daniel Briggs *(points to the south-eastern corner of the square)*: Look at that little column over there, by the statue of Henry Havelock. It's hollow: a hiding place for policemen. The government doesn't want assemblies of people here. That's why the basins around the fountains are so big – to obstruct demonstrations. That doesn't go down well with us Londoners. When we're angry, it's best not to get in our way. But whatever we think of the government, everyone respects Lord Nelson. My gang of builders and me, we'll make sure that nothing bad happens to the admiral and his column.

Holmes: In that case, we will say thank-you, and wish you a good day.

Rückzug nicht sah. Nelson war wirklich ein tatkräftiger und eigenwilliger Mann.

Daniel Briggs: Obrigkeit hat ihn nie eingeschüchtert – das kann uns allen ein Beispiel sein. Und auf dieser Seite sehen Sie eine Szene aus der Seeschlacht bei Abukir. Mit einer schweren Kopfwunde brachten sie ihn in die Kabine. Der Chirurg kam sofort und ließ dafür einen Matrosen liegen, aber Nelson sagte: «Ich warte mit meinen tapferen Kameraden, bis ich an der Reihe bin.» Den rechten Arm verlor er, er war blind auf einem Auge, aber setzte sich immer dem Kampfgetümmel aus. Ich habe gern an seinem Denkmal gearbeitet. Das Volk liebt ihn – auch wenn die Herrschaften, die sich dazu entschieden, Nelson auf diesem Platz eine Ehre zu erweisen, das Volk nicht liebten.

Watson: Wie meinen Sie das?

Daniel Briggs *(zeigt zur Südostecke des Platzes)*: Schauen Sie auf die kleine Säule vor der Statue von Henry Havelock. Sie ist hohl und ist ein Versteck für Polizisten. Die Regierung wünscht hier keine Massenversammlungen. Deshalb sind die Wasserbecken der Brunnen so groß: um Demonstrationen zu verhindern. Wir Londoner halten nicht viel von so etwas. Wenn wir wütend sind, geht man uns besser aus dem Weg. Aber was immer wir von der Regierung halten mögen, Lord Nelson respektieren alle. Meine Truppe und ich sorgen dafür, dass dem Admiral und seiner Säule nichts passiert.

Holmes: Dann bedanken wir uns und wünschen Ihnen einen guten Tag.

8.

Roses and Oranges
(Covent Garden)

Rosen und Apfelsinen
(Covent Garden)

They all thought she was dead; but my father, he kept ladling gin down her throat till she came to so sudden that she bit the bowl off the spoon.

Eliza Doolittle in Pygmalion, George Bernard Shaw

In the Middle Ages Covent Garden was truly a garden, belonging to the monks of Westminster Abbey. After the dissolution of the monasteries in 1540 it came into the possession of the earls of Bedford. A century later, the 4th Earl of Bedford decided to develop the land into a high-class residential district. He engaged Inigo Jones to design a church – and a piazza, the first London square with aristocratic pretensions, for which piazzas in Italy and the Place de Vosges in Paris were the models. Covent Garden did not keep its upmarket residential character for long. A market existed as early as 1654. Soon theatres, taverns and prostitutes moved in. In the 19th century, however, what had become a notorious redlight district was cleaned up, and in 1830 the market halls that still exist today were built. Covent Garden was London's wholesale market for fruit and vegetables until 1974. Its down-to-earth bustle in the very heart of the city made it an irresistible stage and film set: in George Bernard Shaw's play *Pygmalion* and the musical based on it, *My Fair Lady*, Professor Higgins meets the flowerseller Eliza Doolittle under the colonnade of Inigo Jones' church. In 1972 Alfred Hitchcock, whose father was a vegetable trader at Covent Garden, shot his last-but-one film, *Frenzy*, in the market milieu. He knew that the market's days were numbered, and the film consciously captured

Die dachten alle, sie is' tot; aber mein Vater, der hat ihr Gin in die Kehle geschüttet, bis sie zu sich kam – so plötzlich, dass sie den Löffel vom Stiel abbiss.

Eliza Doolittle in ‹Pygmalion›, George Bernard Shaw

Covent Garden war im Mittelalter ein Garten der Mönche von Westminster Abbey. Nach der Auflösung aller Klöster im Jahr 1540 kam das Gelände in den Besitz der Earls of Bedford. Ein knappes Jahrhundert später plante der vierte Earl ein nobles Wohnviertel und beauftragte den Architekten Inigo Jones, eine Kirche zu bauen – und eine Piazza, der erste vornehme Londoner Stadtplatz, für den italienische Piazzen und der Place de Vosges in Paris Modell standen.
Eine feine Wohngegend blieb Covent Garden nicht lang. Bereits 1654 gab es einen Markt. Bald zogen Theater, Tavernen und Prostituierte her. Im 19. Jahrhundert wurde das anrüchige Rotlicht- und Amüsierviertel gesäubert, und 1830 wurden die heute noch existierenden Markthallen errichtet. Covent Garden blieb bis 1974 Londons Großmarkt für Obst und Gemüse. Das geschäftige Treiben normaler Leute im Herzen der Stadt machte es zu einem beliebten Schauplatz für Theater und Film. Im Musical ‹My Fair Lady› lernt Professor Higgins dort die Blumenverkäuferin Eliza Doolittle kennen. Er bringt sie dazu, ihren Londoner «Cockney»-Dialekt abzulegen und wie eine feine Dame zu sprechen. Der Regisseur Alfred Hitchcock, dessen Vater Gemüsehändler in Covent Garden war, drehte 1972 seinen vorletzten Film ‹Frenzy› in diesem kurz danach verschwundenen Milieu, dem

its atmosphere for posterity. Since 1980 Covent Garden has thrived again as a lively district for shopping, dining and entertainment, though no longer with the dubious reputation of past centuries. The piazza around the historic market halls is a magnet for buskers and street entertainers of all kinds.

From Trafalgar Square Holmes and Watson walk up St Martin's Lane and turn right into New Row, which continues as King Street to the square around the market halls. A flower-girl is standing next to one of the columns of St Paul's Church. She is dressed in a brown skirt, a dirty apron and a black straw hat. The roses in her basket look by no means freshly picked.

Holmes: Good day. We would like to speak to you for a moment.

Eliza Doolittle: I ain't done nothin! I'm allowed to sell flowers here. No-one won't stop me.

Holmes *(gives her a coin)***:** I haven't come to accuse you of anything – just to ask about the man who alighted from a hansom cab here and spoke to you yesterday afternoon. That would have been at about four o'clock. A tall, thin man with a black beard.

Eliza Doolittle: A right scrooge he was! Didn't buy a thing. Unfriendly too – a nasty piece of work. He was looking for someone I don't know, so I couldn't help him.

Holmes: You could help us, but I see you don't want to. Perhaps I should enquire where you got those roses. They are a very distinctive kind of rose, called

er damit bewusst ein Denkmal setzte. Seit 1980 blüht Covent Garden wieder als quirliges Viertel für Shopping, Gastronomie und Entertainment – nun aber nicht mehr mit dubiosem Ruf. Die Piazza um die historischen Markthallen herum ist als Magnet für Straßenmusikanten und Gaukler bekannt.

Holmes und Watson gehen von Trafalgar Square in die St Martin's Lane, dann nach rechts in die New Row, die im späteren Verlauf King Street heißt, und erreichen den Platz um die Markthalle. Neben einer der Säulen der St Paul's Church steht eine junge Blumenverkäuferin. Sie trägt einen braunen Rock, eine verschmutzte Schürze und einen schwarzen Strohhut. Die Rosen in ihrem Korb sehen nicht mehr frisch aus.

Holmes: Guten Tag. Wir hätten gern ein Wort mit Ihnen gesprochen.

Eliza Doolittle: Ich habe nichts getan! Ich darf hier Blumen verkaufen. Das kann mir keiner verbieten.

Holmes *(gibt ihr eine Münze)***:** Ich habe nicht vor, Ihnen etwas vorzuwerfen, und möchte lediglich nach dem Mann fragen, der gestern Nachmittag aus einer Droschke stieg und mit Ihnen sprach. Das muss um ungefähr 16 Uhr gewesen sein. Er ist groß und schlank, trägt einen schwarzen Bart.

Eliza Doolittle: Ein richtiger Geizkragen war das! Er kaufte nichts. Unfreundlich war er auch noch – ein übler Typ! Er suchte jemanden, den ich nicht kenne, also konnte ich ihm nicht helfen.

Holmes: Uns könnten Sie helfen, aber wie ich sehe, wollen Sie das nicht. Vielleicht sollte ich mich erkundigen, woher Sie diese Rosen haben. Eine besondere Art, «Templerherz»

"Templar's Heart". I can recognise that blood-red colour at a glance, even though they are half withered. As any rose breeder knows, they are grown in the Temple Garden, and nowhere else. I wonder if anyone stole roses from there two days ago?

Eliza Doolittle: I'm an honest girl, believe me, sir! I really don't know that cove what came here yesterday, cross my heart and hope to die, and I didn't tell him nothing. He was asking after Jim Barnes, and I ain't seen Jim in a long time. I sent him to the fruit stall over there. That's where Jim used to work.

Eliza Doolittle points to a nearby market stall, where a young woman is buying oranges to fill the basket that hangs from her arm. When Holmes and Watson walk over, the woman gives Watson a broad wink, and her pert, pretty face breaks into a grin.

Young woman: Two handsome and well-dressed men who don't seem short of ready money! Now that's a pleasure we don't have every day round here. I know who you are and who you are hoping to find. And I'm more than willing to tell you where to look. But first of all, I'd like to take the opportunity for a little stroll in the company of respectable gentlemen.

Watson: With whom do we have the honour to walk around the piazza?

Young woman: You'll work that out soon enough. I have a reputation, even 200 years on. I was on the stage when I was in my prime, and St Paul's over there was almost a new church. They call it the actors' church, and that's where we'll go now.

heißt die Züchtung, ich erkenne sie an der blutroten Farbe, auch wenn die Blumen halb vertrocknet sind. Wie jeder Rosenzüchter weiß, werden sie im Temple Garden kultiviert und sonst nirgendwo. Ob dort vor zwei Tagen wohl jemand Rosen entwendet hat?

Eliza Doolittle: Ich bin ein ehrliches Mädchen, Glauben Sie mir, Sir! Ich kenne den Kerl wirklich nicht, der gestern hier war, und hab' ihm nichts erzählt, ich schwöre! Er fragte nach Jim Barnes, den hab' ich lange nicht mehr gesehen. Ich schickte ihn zum Obststand drüben. Da hat Jim früher gearbeitet.

Eliza Doolittle zeigt auf einen Stand in der Nähe. Dort füllt eine junge Kundin den Korb, der an ihrem Arm hängt, mit Orangen. Als Holmes und Watson zu ihr hinübergehen, zwinkert sie Watson zu, und auf ihrem hübschen, frechen Gesicht breitet sich ein Grinsen aus.

Junge Frau: Zwei zahlungskräftige und gut aussehende Herren! Wie angenehm, Männer wie Sie sehen wir hier nicht jeden Tag. Ich weiß, wer Sie sind und wen Sie suchen. Und ich sage Ihnen auch gerne, wo Sie ihn finden können. Aber zuerst möchte ich die Gelegenheit nutzen, in der Begleitung zweier Herren ein wenig herumzuspazieren.

Watson: Mit wem haben wir die Ehre, eine Runde um die Piazza zu drehen?

Junge Frau: Sie werden schon früh genug drauf kommen. Ich habe einen gewissen Ruf, auch nach 200 Jahren. In der Blüte meines Lebens stand ich auf der Bühne. Die St Paul's Church dort drüben war damals relativ neu. Man nennt sie die Schauspielerkirche. Dahin gehen wir.

The Earl of Bedford is said to have commissioned Inigo Jones to build a plain church at low cost: something little better than a barn. Jones is supposed to have answered: "I will build you the finest barn in Europe." St Paul's Church has many associations with famous people. The painter J. M. W. Turner and Thomas Arne, composer of *Rule Britannia*, were baptised there. It is the last resting place of many actors, and more are commemorated by a plaque on the wall – Charlie Chaplin, Marie Lloyd, Noel Coward, Ivor Novello, Boris Karloff, Margaret Rutherford, Vivien Leigh and other famous names from the world of show business.

Young woman *(leads the way around the church to the graveyard)*: When we had that dreadful outbreak of the plague in 1665, the first poor woman who died of it in London was buried here. We were all terrified, and to stop it spreading theatre performances were banned, so a lot of us were out of work. Apart from plague victims, in this churchyard there are the graves of some people who had the favour of my Charles. Sir Peter Lely, for example, his court painter. Lely liked to do portraits of duchesses, but he painted me too.

Holmes: You refer to King Charles II as "my Charles"? Then you must be …

Young woman: That's right, Mr Holmes, you've guessed it. I'm Nell Gwyn, royal mistress, at your service. Please don't look so shocked, Dr Watson. Morals were not the same in my time as they are today. Charles – I used to call him my Charles III, by the way, as I was

Der Earl von Bedford soll seinem Architekt Inigo Jones den Auftrag erteilt haben, kostensparend eine schlichte Kirche wie eine Art bessere Scheune zu errichten. Jones antwortete angeblich: «Ich werde Ihnen die großartigste Scheune in Europa bauen.» St Paul's Church ist in langer Tradition mit berühmten Leuten verbunden. Sie war die Taufkirche des Malers J. M. W. Turner und des Komponisten der Rule Britannia, Thomas Arne, und letzte Ruhestätte vieler Schauspieler. Andere ehren Gedenktafeln an der Wand: Charlie Chaplin, Marie Lloyd, Noel Coward, Ivor Novello, Boris Karloff, Margaret Rutherford und viele andere bekannte Namen aus der Welt des Showbusiness.

Junge Frau *(führt sie um die Kirche herum zum Friedhof)*: Als bei uns 1665 die schreckliche Pestepidemie ausbrach, wurde die erste arme Frau, die daran in London starb, hier beerdigt. Wir hatten alle große Angst, und um eine weitere Ausbreitung zu vermeiden, wurden Theateraufführungen verboten, sodass viele von uns arbeitslos waren. Neben der Pestopfer liegen hier einige Männer, die mein Charles mochte. Sir Peter Lely, sein Hofmaler, zum Beispiel. Er porträtierte am liebsten Herzoginnen, mich aber auch.

Holmes: Charles II. nennen Sie «meinen Charles»? Dann sind Sie also …

Junge Frau: Ja, Mr Holmes, Sie haben es erraten. Ich bin Nell Gwyn, königliche Mätresse, zu Diensten. Schauen Sie nicht so schockiert, Dr. Watson, die Sitten waren zu meiner Zeit anders. Charles – ich nannte ihn übrigens immer meinen Charles III., weil ich, bevor ich ihm aufgefal-

on intimate terms with two other gentlemen of that name before I caught the king's eye – had his pleasure with any number of women. Everyone knew it, and he didn't care a jot about that. When Oliver Cromwell and the Puritans ruled the country, you couldn't have any fun at all. They closed the theatres completely, plague or no plague. But then we got a king on the throne again, one who liked to have a good time. Those were golden years for actors, and some other professions too, when wealthy men came to the theatres. I was brought up in Covent Garden. We were poor as church mice, but I had my head screwed on right, and I knew how to make money in the theatres.

Watson: You were an orange-seller. At least, that's what the history books say. That doesn't sound very profitable.

Nell Gwyn: I did sell oranges, but that wasn't the main thing. The cavaliers who bought my oranges in the theatre needed someone to pass messages and love letters to the actresses. I made myself useful as a go-between, and the gentlemen showed their appreciation. I always knew how to deal with men, and it wasn't long before I got the chance to go on stage myself. I'll show you where I performed.

From the church they walk past the market towards the Royal Opera House.

Holmes: You weren't an opera singer, as far as I am aware.

Nell Gwyn: I could sing very well, but I didn't tread

len bin, intime Beziehungen mit zwei Herren mit demselben Namen geführt hatte – hatte natürlich seinen Spaß mit zahllosen Frauen, das wusste jeder, und es war ihm egal, wer's wusste. Als Oliver Cromwell und die Puritaner das Land regierten, war kein Spaß erlaubt. Sie ließen die Theater alle schließen, Pest hin oder her. Dann bekamen wir wieder einen König, der sich gerne amüsierte. Für Schauspieler und andere, die bestimmte Berufe ausübten, brachen goldene Zeiten an, als wohlhabende Männer in die Theater kamen. Ich bin hier in Covent Garden aufgewachsen – bettelarm, aber nicht auf den Kopf gefallen. Ich wusste, wie ich in den Theatern Geld verdienen konnte.

Watson: Sie haben Apfelsinen verkauft. So steht es zumindest in den Geschichtsbüchern. Das klingt nicht sehr einträglich.

Nell Gwyn: Ich habe Apfelsinen verkauft, aber darum ging es nicht wirklich. Die Kavaliere, die sie mir im Theater abkauften, brauchten jemanden, der Botschaften und Liebesbriefe an die Schauspielerinnen überbrachte. Ich machte mich als Mittlerin nützlich, und die Herren waren dankbar und zeigten sich erkenntlich. Ich wusste schon immer Männer um den kleinen Finger zu wickeln, und bekam bald meine Chance, selber auf der Bühne zu stehen. Kommen Sie mit, ich zeige Ihnen, wo ich aufgetreten bin.

Von der Kirche gehen sie an den Markthallen vorbei zu dem Royal Opera House.

Holmes: Opernsängerin waren Sie aber nicht, soweit ich weiß.

Nell Gwyn: Singen konnte ich schon, aber hier stand ich

the boards here, so we're not stopping. We'll go on to Russell Street, ahead of us. The king licensed two companies. Our rivals, the Duke's Company, played here in Covent Garden; we were the King's Company, and our theatre was over there in Drury Lane.

Watson: It was the King's Company? That was how you won the royal favour?

Nell Gwyn: I was one of the very first women who acted. Before that, they had boys to play the female parts. When pretty girls finally appeared in the theatres, the public couldn't get enough of it. The theatre managers made sure our charms were on display. There were plenty of amorous scenes in the dramas. If the respectable ladies of your acquaintance today could have heard the repartee, Dr Watson, they'd blush bright red. But Charles loved coarse jokes, the naughtier the better. When he came to the theatre, I could feel his royal eye roving over me. But don't think it was just my looks that got noticed. I made people laugh. I could improvise, and everyone praised me for my quick wit – yes, me, the girl from the gutter. I won the respect of educated men.

Nell Gwyn takes them to the corner of Russell Street and Catherine Street, where a long colonnade flanks the Theatre Royal, Drury Lane.

The present theatre, the fourth on the site, was built in 1812. From 1664 Nell Gwyn made appearances in the first of the four, which burned to the ground in 1672. The rebuilt theatre made stage history. Its man-

nicht auf der Bühne, deshalb gehen wir weiter zur Russell Street. Der König hat zwei Theatertruppen lizenziert. Unsere Rivalen, die Duke's Company, spielten in Covent Garden; wir, die King's Company, drüben in der Drury Lane.

Watson: Die King's Company? So kamen sie in die Gunst des Königs?

Nell Gwyn: Ich war eine der ersten Schauspielerinnen. Vorher spielten Knaben die weiblichen Rollen. Als es endlich hübsche Mädchen zu sehen gab, war das Publikum ganz heiß darauf. Die Theaterdirektoren gingen sicher, dass wir unsere Reize zeigten. Es gab viele Liebesszenen in den Stücken. Und könnten die feinen Damen, die Sie heute kennen, Mr Watson, unsere Wortgefechte hören, dann würden sie erröten. Die zotigen Witze waren sehr nach Charles' Geschmack, je unanständiger, desto besser. Wann immer er ins Theater kam, konnte ich seine Blicke spüren. Aber ich fiel nicht nur auf, weil ich gut aussah, ich brachte die Leute auch zum Lachen. Ich konnte improvisieren, und alle lobten meine Schlagfertigkeit – ja, ich, das Mädchen aus der Gosse, gewann den Respekt gebildeter Männer.

Nell Gwyn führt sie an die Ecke Russell Street/Catherine Street, zu dem Säulengang des Theatre Royal, Drury Lane.

Das 1812 errichtete Theater ist das vierte an dieser Stelle. Im ersten trat Nell Gwyn ab 1664 auf, aber bereits 1672 fiel es einem Brand zum Opfer. Der Wiederaufbau schrieb Theatergeschichte. Zu den Direktoren

agers included David Garrick, the greatest actor of his day, and the playwright Richard Brinsley Sheridan. *God Save the Queen* was played here in public for the first time. In 1791 a large new theatre replaced it. This building was hailed as the world's first with effective precautions against fire: water tanks, columns of iron instead of wood, and an iron safety curtain. It burned down within a few years. The fourth building, now owned by Sir Andrew Lloyd Webber's company, also has a distinguished history. It was the venue for the premiere and over 2,000 performances of *My Fair Lady*. Among the notable features of the house are two royal boxes and a ghost that glides into the auditorium through the left-hand wall.

Nell Gwyn: This is where I leave you, gentlemen. I don't know the tall, hollow-cheeked man with the beard who came to the fruit stall yesterday and asked for Jim Barnes. But I do know Jim. He's short and stocky, with a mop of red hair. He used to be employed on the market, but he's happier if he can earn money fast without much effort, and he'll do anyone's dirty work. If you want to speak to him, the place to look is a tavern on Fleet Street: Ye Olde Cheshire Cheese.

She disappears through the wall of the theatre. Holmes and Watson exchange glances, then make their way along Catherine Street to Aldwych. This road in turn leads them in a curve down to The Strand, where they turn right and walk a short distance.

hier gehörten der größte Schauspieler seiner Zeit, David Garrick, und der Bühnenautor Richard Brinsley Sheridan. Hier wurde zum ersten Mal ‹God Save The Queen›, die britische Nationalhymne, gespielt. 1791 wurde das zweite durch ein neues, großes Theater ersetzt. Es wurde als erstes gegen Feuer geschütztes Theater der Welt angepriesen – mit Wassertanks, Säulen aus Eisen statt Holz und einem eisernen Vorhang – und brannte nach wenigen Jahren ab. Auch der vierte Theaterbau – heutiger Besitzer: Andrew Lloyd Webber – hat viele Sternstunden erlebt, z. B. war er der Spielort für die Premiere von ‹My Fair Lady›, das über 2000-mal aufgeführt wurde. Die Besonderheiten des Hauses sind zwei königliche Logen und ein Gespenst, das durch die linke Wand in den Zuschauerraum hineingleitet.

Nell Gwyn: Hier verlasse ich Sie, meine Herren. Den großen hageren Mann mit Bart, der gestern am Obststand nach Jim Barnes fragte, kenne ich nicht. Den Jim schon. Er ist klein und breit und hat rote Haare. Er hat früher am Markt gearbeitet, aber er verdient sein Geld lieber auf schnelle Art und Weise und erledigt für jeden die Drecksarbeit. Wenn Sie ihn suchen, gehen Sie zur Taverne Ye Olde Cheshire Cheese in der Fleet Street.

Sie verschwindet durch die Außenmauer des Theaters. Holmes und Watson tauschen Blicke aus und begeben sich dann über die Catherine Street zu der Straße Aldwych, die sie in einem Bogen zu The Strand führt. Dort gehen sie ein kurzes Stück nach rechts.

9.

Celebrities and Scandal
(The Savoy Hotel)

Prominenz und Skandal
(Savoy Hotel)

There is only one thing in the world worse than being talked about, and that is not being talked about.

From *The Picture of Dorian Gray*, Oscar Wilde

When the Savoy Hotel opened in 1889, it was London's first luxury hotel, managed by César Ritz with his partner, the legendary chef Auguste Escoffier, who ruled the kitchens. Since their time the Savoy has accommodated a cosmopolitan clientele of the rich and famous, and countless stories are told of the goings-on there. In 1905 the American millionaire George A. Kessler had the Thames Foyer flooded to a depth of five feet for a Venice-themed party at which dinner was served on a gondola. In the 1920s the modish Art Deco interior and a reputation for the best cocktails in London drew high society. George Gershwin played the world premiere of his *Rhapsody in Blue* at the Savoy. Errol Flynn and Katherine Hepburn, Josephine Baker and Coco Chanel were among the guests.

The outbreak of the Second World War did not put an end the procession of celebrities passing through the doors. Winston Churchill often ate lunch there with his cabinet, and after the war the young Princess Elizabeth and her future husband Philip appeared in public together for the first time in the Savoy Hotel.

The management noted the wishes of prominent guests on cards, which were filed for future reference. As the cards have survived, we know that

Denn es gibt nur eines, das schlimmer ist, als dass über einen geredet wird, nämlich, dass nicht über einen geredet wird.

Aus ‹Das Bildnis des Dorian Gray›, Oscar Wilde

Das Savoy Hotel öffnete 1889 als Londons erste Luxus-
herberge seine Pforten. Geleitet wurde es von César
Ritz mit seinem Partner, und in der Küche regierte der
legendäre Koch Auguste Escoffier. Seit diesen Tagen
beherbergt das Savoy die Reichen und Berühmten der
Welt. Zahllose Geschichten werden über das dortige
Treiben erzählt. 1905 ließ der amerikanische Millionär
George A. Kessler für eine Feier mit dem Thema
«Venedig» das Thames Foyer 1,5 Meter tief mit Wasser
fluten, sodass Dinner in einer Gondel serviert wurden.
In den 1920ern machten die Einrichtung im Art Déco-
Stil und die als unübertroffen geltenden Cocktails das
Hotel zum Society-Treff. George Gershwin spielte die
Weltpremiere seiner ‹Rhapsody in Blue› im Savoy. Zu
den Gästen zählten Errol Flynn und Katharine Hepburn,
Josephine Baker und Coco Chanel.
Auch der Ausbruch des Zweiten Weltkriegs ließ die
Berühmtheiten nicht fortbleiben. Winston Churchill
kam häufig mit seinem Kabinett zum Mittagessen
dorthin. Nach dem Krieg zeigten sich Prinzessin
Elizabeth und ihr zukünftiger Mann Philip hier zum
ersten Mal gemeinsam in der Öffentlichkeit.
Die Wünsche prominenter Stammgäste notierte die
Hotelleitung auf Karteikarten, die zum späteren Nach-
schlagen aufbewahrt wurden. Da die Karten noch er-
halten sind, wissen wir, dass Marlene Dietrich sofort

Marlene Dietrich required a dozen pink roses and a bottle of Dom Perignon champagne on her arrival. Other cards record the preferences of Sophia Loren, Marilyn Monroe and Louis Armstrong. The actor Richard Harris, whose card specifies the exact temperature of his porridge, lived in the Savoy for a good part of the last years of his life. When, shortly before his death, he was carried out on a stretcher, he summoned the strength to call out to diners in the hotel restaurant: "It was the food." The closeness of the hotel to the river Thames gave rise to one of the strangest stories. Two guests, passionate fly fishermen, wagered whether it would be possible to cast a salmon line into the river from the roof of the Savoy. They found an expert angler who declared himself willing to try the feat, on the condition that he was securely tied to a chimney. Early one Sunday morning police closed the Embankment to traffic for a few minutes, and the attempt was successful. Later the great violinist Jascha Heifetz once climbed out onto the hotel roof, not for fishing but for his musical education: he needed a place where he could take bagpipe lessons undisturbed.

The name of the hotel originated in the 13th century, when Henry III gave land between The Strand and the river to Peter of Savoy, his queen's uncle. Peter built a palace there, and the name survived through the ages until the construction of the Savoy Theatre in 1881. A few years later Richard D'Oyly Carte, the owner of the theatre and impresario of comic ope-

nach der Ankunft ein Dutzend pinkfarbene Rosen und eine Flasche Dom-Perignon-Champagner wünschte. Weitere Kärtchen hielten die Vorlieben von Sophia Loren, Marilyn Monroe und Louis Armstrong fest. Der Schauspieler Richard Harris – sein Kärtchen schrieb die exakte Temperatur des Haferbreis vor – wohnte während seiner letzten Lebensjahre im Hotel. Als er kurz vor seinem Tod erkrankte und auf einer Bahre hinausgetragen wurde, fand er noch die Kraft, den Gästen im Restaurant zuzurufen: «Es war das Essen.»

Die Nähe zur Themse führte zu einem der merkwürdigsten Ereignisse in der Hotelgeschichte. Zwei Gäste, beide begeisterte Fliegenfischer, wetteten gegeneinander, ob es möglich wäre, vom Hoteldach eine Lachsrute in den Fluss auszuwerfen. Unter der Bedingung, dass man ihn an einen Kamin auf dem Dach festband, erklärte sich ein erfahrener Angler bereit, den Versuch zu wagen. Früh an einem Sonntagmorgen hielt ein Polizist an der Uferstraße für einige Minuten den Verkehr auf, und der Wurf gelang. Später kletterte einmal der Geigenvirtuose Jascha Heifetz auf das Hoteldach, nicht zum Fischen, sondern für seine musikalische Weiterbildung: Er wollte ungestört Dudelsackunterricht nehmen.

Der Name des Hotels stammt aus dem 13. Jahrhundert. König Henry III. schenkte dem Onkel seiner Königin, Peter von Savoyen, ein Grundstück zwischen The Strand und der Themse, wo Peter einen Palast baute. Der Name überstand den Wandel der Zeit bis zum Bau des Savoy Theatre im Jahr 1881. Einige Jahre später entschied sich Richard D'Oyly Carte, der Besitzer

ras, decided to build a hotel next door. Savoy Court, the short cul-de-sac leading to the theatre and hotel from The Strand, is one further oddity of the site: it is the only road in the United Kingdom where cars drive on the right.

Holmes and Watson cross The Strand to enter Savoy Court and stop there to take a look at the hotel.

Holmes: The prime minister believes that the threat expressed in the anonymous letter is directed against a major building. But what if a prominent person is the target? The letter is not absolutely explicit about that. He told me there are no high-ranking guests of state in London at present, but is it possible that members of a European royal family are staying here privately? If so, the Savoy Hotel would be the suitable accommodation. I was once able to assist the manager, Mr Ritz, in the remarkable case of the Princess of F, and spared him a good deal of embarrassment. I'm sure he will be willing to help us.

The porter recognises the great detective and touches his top hat. At the reception desk Holmes announces that he would like to speak to César Ritz, who appears without delay.

Ritz: Mr Holmes, Dr Watson, welcome to our hotel. What can I do for you?

Holmes: We have received information about a possible threat to prominent persons. Do you have among your guests representatives of a royal house?

Ritz: The Prince of Wales dined here yesterday evening,

und Direktor des Theaters, nebenan ein Hotel zu errichten. Die kurze Stichstraße, Savoy Court, die von The Strand zum Theater und Hotel führt, stellt eine weitere Eigentümlichkeit dar: Es ist die einzige Straße des Vereinigten Königreichs mit Rechtsverkehr.

Holmes und Watson überqueren The Strand zum Savoy Court und stoppen vor dem Hotel.

Holmes: Der Premierminister meint, dass sich die in dem anonymen Brief geäußerte Drohung gegen ein wichtiges Bauwerk richtet. Aber was, wenn eine berühmte Person das Ziel ist? Aus dem Schreiben ging nichts Genaues hervor. Er erzählte mir, dass sich zurzeit keine Staatsgäste von hohem Rang in der Stadt aufhielten, aber vielleicht halten sich königliche Hoheiten hier privat auf? Wenn ja, dann am ehesten im Savoy Hotel. Ich konnte einmal dem Hotelmanager, Mr Ritz, im kuriosen Fall der Fürstin von F. helfen und ersparte ihm Unannehmlichkeiten. Er wird uns bereitwillig helfen, da bin ich mir sicher.

Der Portier erkennt den großen Detektiv und lupft seinen Zylinder. Am Empfang meldet Holmes, dass er mit César Ritz zu sprechen wünsche, der umgehend erscheint.

César Ritz: Mr Holmes, Dr. Watson, ich begrüße Sie in unserem Haus. Was kann ich für Sie tun?
Holmes: Wir haben Hinweise, dass wichtigen Personen Gefahr drohen könnte. Sind königliche Hoheiten heute unter den Gästen?
Ritz: Gestern Abend dinierte der Prinz of Wales hier, aber er

but he seldom stays the night. The actress Sarah Bernhardt is occupying a suite here at the moment, and she is certainly regal. Members of the kingdom's noblest families come to our restaurant, as Monsieur Escoffier is the world's finest chef. Just a few years ago it was unthinkable for a duchess to be seen dining in public, but Auguste and I have succeeded in changing that. Of course we take discreet measures to ensure the safety of our guests, so that they can feel at their ease.

Holmes: But there are no heads of state here at present, or other persons whose well-being might be important to the government?

Ritz: Not at the moment, unusually.

Watson: If you don't mind me asking, what is it, apart from the quality of your restaurant, that makes this hotel so attractive to high society?

Ritz: The owner, Mr D'Oyly Carte, often visits America, and was impressed by the modern luxuries there. He decided it was time to open such an institution in London, with all the facilities that persons of distinction expect. That was long overdue. Perhaps you can recall the opening of our hotel. It caused a sensation. We were the first in London to have electric lighting, and a private bathroom with hot and cold running water for the majority of the rooms. We also have electrically operated lifts, so that even the most refined guests can take a room on the upper floors and enjoy the view.

Watson: Ah, yes, I have heard of those "ascending chambers". Are they really safe, and a suitable means of transport for ladies from the best social circles?

übernachtet selten bei uns. Die Schauspielerin Sarah Bernhardt hat zurzeit eine Suite, und man kann sie als königlich bezeichnen. Mitglieder des Hochadels sind ständig im Restaurant zu finden – Monsieur Escoffier ist bekanntlich der weltbeste Koch. Vor einigen Jahren war es noch undenkbar, dass eine Herzogin in öffentlichen Räumen speist – aber Auguste und ich haben das geändert. Wir treffen natürlich diskrete Sicherheitsmaßnahmen, damit sich unsere Gäste wohlfühlen können.

Holmes: Aber es wohnen momentan keine Staatsoberhäupter oder andere Personen, deren Sicherheit Bedeutung für das Empire hat, im Hause?

Ritz: Ausnahmsweise nicht.

Watson: Bitte verzeihen Sie die Frage: Von der Qualität Ihrer Küche abgesehen, welche Vorzüge sind es, die so prominente Gäste an diesem Hotel schätzen?

Ritz: Der Hotelbesitzer, Mr D'Oyly Carte, ist oft in Amerika, wo ihn der Luxus in den modernen Hotels beeindruckte. Er beschloss, dass es an der Zeit war, solch ein Haus in London zu bauen, mit allen Annehmlichkeiten, die Personen von Rang und Namen erwarten. Das war längst überfällig. Vielleicht erinnern Sie sich, welche Sensation die Eröffnung unseres Hotels war. Wir waren die Ersten in London mit elektrischer Beleuchtung, und einem eigenen Bad mit fließend heißem und kaltem Wasser für die meisten Gästezimmer. Wir haben auch elektrisch betriebene Personenaufzüge, und so kann sogar das feinste Klientel Zimmer in den oberen Etagen belegen und den Ausblick genießen.

Watson: Von den «aufsteigenden Kammern» habe ich gehört. Sie sind auch wirklich sicher und für die Beförderung von Damen aus gehobenen Kreisen geeignet?

Ritz: Come along, I'll show you the view of the Thames from one of the upper floors.

He takes Holmes and Watson to the top floor and opens the door to a room.

Ritz: Gentlemen, what do you think of this panorama? A French painter stayed with us for several weeks. His name is Claude Monet. He painted the river and Waterloo Bridge from this very window.

Holmes *(takes his magnifying glass from his pocket)***:** The curtains reveal that Monsieur Monet liked the colours of sunset. However, your residents will probably not notice these tiny splashes of paint.

César Ritz leads Holmes and Watson back to the ground floor.

Ritz: Are you hungry, Mr Holmes? Auguste has just invented a new sweet delicacy especially for Mrs Nellie Melba, the opera singer. It consists of vanilla ice cream, peaches and raspberry sauce. He has called it "peach Melba" in her honour. Mrs Melba was singing at Covent Garden in *Lohengrin*, and was delighted when the dessert was served in a swan carved from ice.

Holmes: Many thanks, but we have to continue our investigations without delay. Before we leave, I beg forgiveness for asking a question on a rather delicate subject. It relates to the distressing scandal of Mr Oscar Wilde and Lord Alfred Douglas. The newspapers reported that some of the unseemly events took place in your hotel. Have you received any threats in connection with this matter?

Ritz: Kommen Sie mit, ich zeige Ihnen den Blick auf die
   Themse von einer der oberen Etagen aus.

Er fährt mit Holmes und Watson in das oberste Stockwerk
und öffnet die Tür zu einem der Zimmer.

Ritz: Was halten Sie von diesem Panorama, meine Herren?
   Ein französischer Maler residierte mehrere Wochen bei
   uns. Claude Monet ist sein Name. An diesem Fenster malte
   er den Fluss und die Waterloo Bridge.
Holmes *(holt seine Lupe aus der Tasche)*: Die Gardinen
   verraten Monsieurs Monets Vorliebe für die Farben der
   Sonnenuntergänge. Aber Gäste werden diese feinen Farb-
   spritzer kaum bemerken.

César Ritz führt Holmes und Watson zurück in das Erdge-
schoss.

Ritz: Haben Sie Hunger, Mr Holmes? Auguste hat eigens
   für die Opernsängerin Nellie Melba einen neuen Nach-
   tisch aus Vanilleeis, Pfirsich und Himbeerpüree erfunden:
   «Pfirsich Melba» nennt er es ihr zu Ehren. Mrs Melba
   sang in Covent Garden im ‹Lohengrin› und war sehr an-
   getan, als er ihr dieses Dessert in einem Schwan aus Eis
   kredenzte.
Holmes: Vielen Dank, aber wir müssen unsere Untersuchun-
   gen umgehend an anderer Stelle fortsetzen. Bevor wir gehen, bitte ich um Verzeihung, wenn ich eine etwas heikle
   Frage stelle. Es betrifft diesen unangenehmen Skandal um
   Mr Oscar Wilde und Lord Alfred Douglas. Die Zeitungen
   schrieben, dass sich diese ungebührlichen Dinge teilweise
   in Ihrem Hotel abspielten. Haben Sie in diesem Zusam-
   menhang irgendwelche Drohungen erhalten?

Watson: Holmes! You mean the author of plays who was disgraced and given a prison sentence last month for gross indecency. That is an unmentionable matter!

Ritz *(lowers his voice):* It's true that Oscar Wilde and the young Lord Alfred often stayed here. I had not the slightest idea that the crimes he was accused of were being committed under this very roof … well, you will understand how embarrassing this is. We made sure that the staff of the hotel testified in the trial against Wilde, to emphasise that the Savoy Hotel refuses to tolerate any unnatural acts. And no, we have received no threats related to this matter. Mr Holmes, I should be most obliged if this matter could be closed. As you are clearly in a hurry, I'll accompany you to the exit.

Watson: Holmes! Sie reden von dem in Ungnade gefallenen Schriftsteller, der letzten Monat eine Gefängnisstrafe wegen Unzucht erhielt. Eine höchst unanständige Sache!

Ritz *(flüstert)*: Es stimmt, dass Oscar Wilde und der junge Lord oft unsere Gäste waren. Ich hatte nicht den geringsten Verdacht, dass diese Delikte, wegen denen er angeklagt war, unter unserem Dach stattfanden ... na ja, Sie verstehen, wie unangenehm es ist. Bedienstete des Hotels waren Zeugen im Prozess gegen Wilde – dafür haben wir gesorgt und möchten zeigen, dass unser Haus unmoralische Handlungen nicht toleriert. Und nein, Drohungen haben wir keine bekommen. Ich wäre Ihnen verbunden, Mr Holmes, wenn davon nicht mehr gesprochen würde. Ich bringe Sie zum Ausgang, da Sie es offensichtlich eilig haben.

10.

A Poet and a Knight
(The Temple)

Ein Dichter und ein Ritter
(The Temple)

There are, still, worse places than the Temple,
on a sultry day, for basking in the sun, or resting
idly in the shade. There is yet a drowsiness in
its courts, and a dreamy dulness in its trees and
gardens; those who pace its lanes and squares
may yet hear the echoes of their footsteps on
the sounding stones, and read upon its gates, in
passing from the tumult of the Strand or Fleet
Street, "Who enters here leaves noise behind."
There is still the plash of falling water in fair
Fountain Court …

From *Barnaby Rudge*, Charles Dickens

The Middle Temple and Inner Temple are two of the
four Inns of Court, which emerged in the 14th century as law schools. The area where for hundreds of
years barristers have lived and worked, and students
of law have learned, is a labyrinth of alleys and courtyards, a secluded and quiet place amidst the roar of
the city. In order to be admitted to the bar – that is, to
be allowed to plead in higher courts – students have
to be members of one of the Inns of Court and dine
in the hall there on a specified number of occasions.
Many legal practices still have their chambers in the
Inns of Court.
To the east of Middle Temple Lane are the buildings
of the Inner Temple, which can be identified by the
sign of the winged horse Pegasus, and to the west
are the courtyards of the Middle Temple, which has a
lamb and flag as its symbol. The grounds of the Tem-

Es gibt schlechtere Orte als den Temple, wenn man sich an einem schwülen Tag in der Sonne aalen oder sich müßig im Schatten ausruhen will. Seine Höfe wirken immer noch verschlafen, und seine Bäume und Gärten strahlen eine verträumte Entrücktheit aus. Wer über seine Gassen und Plätze geht, kann noch das Echo seiner Schritte auf den widerhallenden Steinen hören und, wenn er aus dem Trubel des Strand und der Fleet Street kommt, kann er an seinen Toren lesen: ‹Wer hier eintritt, lässt den Lärm hinter sich.› Immer noch hört man das Plätschern des fallenden Wassers im hübschen Brunnenhof …

Aus ‹Barnaby Rudge›, Charles Dickens

Der Middle Temple und der Inner Temple sind zwei der vier Inns of Court, die im 14. Jahrhundert als eine Art Universität für angehende Juristen entstanden. Diese Gegend, wo Jurastudenten jahrhundertelang lernten, wo Rechtsanwälte ihre Arbeits- und Wohnräume hatten, ist ein Wirrwarr von Gassen und Höfen, eine Ruhezone mitten in der Großstadt. Um die Zulassung als «Barrister» zu erhalten, das heißt, um Plädoyers vor höheren Gerichten halten zu dürfen, müssen Studenten bis heute Mitglied eines Inns werden und dort eine bestimmte Anzahl pro Semester speisen. Zahlreiche Anwaltskanzleien nutzen noch immer Räumlichkeiten in den Inns of Court. Östlich der Middle Temple Lane liegen die Gebäude des Inner Temple, leicht zu erkennen an einem Symbol mit dem geflügelten Pferd Pegasus, und westlich die Höfe des Middle Temple, dessen Zeichen ein Lamm mit Standarte ist. Der Temple-Bezirk ist an Wochentagen

ple are open on weekdays and, for limited hours, on Sundays. The opening times of the Temple Church can be found at www.templechurch.com.

Holmes and Watson walk east along the Strand, passing the churches of St Mary-le-Strand and St Clement Danes, to reach the place where the city gate known as Temple Bar stood until 1878. It was the boundary between Westminster and the City of London, marked after demolition by a monument in the middle of the road consisting of a tall, decorated plinth and a fearsome-looking griffin. The heads of rebels were once set on spikes on the top of Temple Bar. On the north side of the road, the 19th-century Gothic Revival style of the Royal Courts of Justice is an extravagant reference to the ancient origins of the legal system. Opposite them, on the right just a few paces beyond the memorial to Temple Bar, a stone gateway with black double doors bears the date 1684. Holmes and Watson enter through the side door and find themselves in a narrow street named Middle Temple Lane.

Watson: Holmes, why do you think the mysterious passenger in Mays' hansom cab came to the Temple? Could he do anything here that would endanger the national interest?

Holmes: The Temple has been the legal quarter for 600 years. Great lawyers have lived and worked here: John Hampden, who defended the rights of Parliament against Charles I's assertion of absolute royal authority, and Sir William Blackstone, whose

tagsüber und sonntags eingeschränkt für Besucher geöffnet. (Für die wechselnden Öffnungszeiten der Kirche
siehe www.templechurch.com)

Holmes und Watson setzen ihren Weg entlang The Strand
in Richtung Osten fort. Vorbei an den Kirchen St Mary-
le-Strand und St Clement Dane erreichen sie die Stelle,
wo bis 1878 das «Temple Bar» genannte Stadttor die
Grenze zwischen Westminster und der City of London
markierte. Seit seiner Zerstörung erinnert ein Denkmal in
der Straßenmitte mit einem hohen verzierten Sockel, auf
dem ein furchterregender Greif prangt. Früher wurden
die aufgespießten Köpfe von Rebellen auf dem Tor auf-
gereiht. Auf der linken Seite stehen Gerichtsgebäude, die
Royal Courts of Justice, in Erinnerung an die einstigen
Anfänge der Justiz im neugotischen Stil des 19. Jahrhunderts gehalten. Gegenüber, nur wenige Schritte hinter
Temple Bar, befindet sich rechts ein in Stein gefasster
Eingang mit zwei schwarzen Torflügeln, darüber das
Jahresdatum 1684. Holmes und Watson gehen durch den
Seiteneingang und finden sich in einer engen Gasse mit
dem Namen Middle Temple Lane wieder.

Watson: Was glauben Sie, Holmes, warum unser geheimnis-
voller Droschkenpassagier zum Temple wollte? Könnte
er hier etwas anrichten, das die Interessen des Landes be-
droht?

Holmes: Seit 600 Jahren ist der Temple das Justizviertel. Große Rechtsgelehrte haben hier gewirkt: John Hampden, der
die Rechte des Parlaments gegen die Durchsetzung einer
absoluten Monarchie von Charles I. verteidigt hat, und
Sir William Blackstone, dessen Werke eine tragende Säule

scholarly works are a pillar of our legal system and a foundation of the American constitution. An attack on the Temple would be an insult to law and order, a challenge to our freedom. And besides, the buildings here are important and beautiful, and rich in historic associations. That's where we're going now: to Middle Temple Hall and the Temple Church.

Watson: Your learning never fails to impress me, Holmes! I have no doubt you can also tell me why this district is called The Temple.

Holmes: That's elementary, my dear Watson. This place once belonged to the Knights Templar. They originally protected pilgrims to the Holy Land, and had their base on the Temple Mount in Jerusalem. Their main English base, a kind of monastery, was here. After the dissolution of the Templar order, lawyers established their schools and chambers on the site.

From Middle Temple Lane, Holmes and Watson turn right into Fountain Court, where they see Middle Temple Hall and, in front of the hall, a balding middle-aged man whose remaining hair is combed back straight and smooth. He has a wide but thin moustache, and is conspicuously dressed in criss-crossed yellow garters.

Watson: Bless my soul, Holmes! I can hardly believe my eyes. That man's face is exactly like the portraits of Shakespeare.

Holmes: I wasn't expecting to meet anyone else on this spot. I only hope he'll be concise and to the point, for once. We have no time today for long soliloquies.

Shakespeare: Well met, Mr Holmes and Dr Watson.

unseres Rechtssystems und eine Grundlage der amerikanischen Verfassung sind. Ein Anschlag auf den Temple wäre ein Angriff auf Recht und Ordnung, ein Angriff auf unsere Freiheit. Außerdem sind die Gebäude hier nicht nur schön und wichtig, sondern auch von historischer Bedeutung. Dort gehen wir hin, zur Middle Temple Hall und zur Temple Church.

Watson: Was Sie nicht alles wissen, Holmes – ich bin immer wieder beeindruckt! Sie werden mir sicher auch sagen können, warum diese Gegend The Temple heißt.

Holmes: Selbstverständlich, mein lieber Watson. Das Gelände gehörte einst den Tempelrittern. Ursprünglich beschützten sie Pilger auf dem Weg ins Heilige Land und hatten ihren Sitz in Jerusalem. In England hatten sie hier ihren Hauptsitz, eine Art Kloster. Nach der Auflösung des Ordens etablierten die Juristen ihre Schulen und Kammern.

Von der Middle Temple Lane gehen Holmes und Watson nach rechts in den Fountain Court und stehen vor der Middle Temple Hall. Vor dem Gebäude sehen sie einen Mann mittleren Alters mit einer Halbglatze, zurückgekämmten glatten Haaren und einem breiten, dünnen Oberlippenbart. Das Auffälligste an ihm sind die mit Bändern umwickelten gelben Strümpfe, die er trägt.

Watson: Großer Gott, Holmes! Ich traue meinen Augen kaum. Das Gesicht des Mannes sieht genauso aus wie auf den Porträts von Shakespeare.

Holmes: Niemand anderen habe ich erwartet, an dieser Stelle zu treffen. Ich hoffe, er wird sich ausnahmsweise kurzfassen. Für lange Monologe fehlt uns heute die Zeit.

William Shakespeare: Seien Sie gegrüßt, Mr Holmes und

I greet the great detective and his illustrious chronicler!

"Be not afraid of greatness:
Some are born great, Some achieve greatness,
And some have greatness thrust upon them."
Like yourselves, I was not born great, but had to
strive to make my mark in the world. Of course you
recognised those lines from my play *Twelfth Night*?
We performed it here for the first time at Candlemas
in 1602. This hall is the scene of one of my most
memorable triumphs.

Watson: But this isn't a theatre, it's a dining hall for
lawyers.

Shakespeare: Entertainments were often staged in Middle Temple Hall. Especially in the weeks of merriment
after Christmas. Until Candlemas a Prince of Love
ruled here in the Temple. The young lawyers loved to
celebrate, and they had a pleasing enthusiasm for literature. Many of them composed poetry and engaged
in literary disputes. The Temple was renowned for its
festivities. The hall was full to bursting point, the ale
flowed, the mood was noisy and unruly. Our audiences wanted to roar with laughter, shout and poke
fun at the figures on the stage. Jokes were called for,
the bawdier the better, but at the same time an author
had to demonstrate his learning. So I put in references to the events of the day, and little puns using legal
terms – wit and allusions that only the well-informed
would understand. The learned lawyers understood,
of course. They felt flattered, and laughed even louder
than before. But if the play didn't find their favour,

Dr. Watson. Ich heiße den berühmten Detektiv und seinen illustren Chronist willkommen!

«Einige werden groß geboren
Andere arbeiten sich zu Größe empor.
Und andern wird sie zugeworfen.»

Wie auch Ihnen war mir nichts in die Wiege gelegt, und ich musste mich anstrengen, um mir einen Namen in dieser Welt zu machen. Sie erkennen die Zeilen aus meinem Stück ‹Was ihr wollt› bestimmt? Wir haben es hier an Mariä Lichtmess im Jahre 1602 uraufgeführt. Diese Halle ist also der Schauplatz einer meiner größten Erfolge.

Watson: Hier ist aber kein Theater, sondern eine Speisehalle von Rechtsgelehrten.

Shakespeare: Es gab häufig Unterhaltungen in der Middle Temple Hall. Vor allem in den närrischen Wochen nach Weihnachten – damals herrschte hier bis Mariä Lichtmess der Prinz der Liebe. Die jungen Juristen feierten gerne und waren literaturbegeistert. Viele schrieben selbst Gedichte und diskutierten über Literatur. Der Temple war berühmt für Festlichkeiten. Der Saal war brechend voll, Bier floss in rauen Mengen, und es ging laut und wild zu. Unser Publikum wollte lachen und spotten, grölen und sich über die Figuren auf der Bühne lustig machen. Witze waren ausdrücklich erwünscht, so zotig wie möglich, dabei musste ein Autor aber auch beweisen, dass er belesen und klug war. Also nahm ich Bezug auf das Tagesgeschehen und machte Wortspiele mit juristischen Begriffen – Anspielungen, die nur gut unterrichtete Zuhörer verstehen, und die gebildeten Anwälte taten das natürlich. Alle waren geschmeichelt und brüllten noch lauter vor Lachen. Aber wenn das Stück nicht gut ankam, waren wir Spieler nicht

then we players were not to be envied. They threw
bones and tankards, and things worse than that.

Holmes: This is all most interesting, Mr Shakespeare,
and we are especially privileged to hear it from the
lips of the Great Bard. However, we have come
here with a purpose, and must take a close look at
Middle Temple Hall.

Shakespeare *(leads them inside)*: Then come with me.
Look at the wonderful double hammer-beam roof.
No troupe of players could wish for a finer backdrop
than this hall! And have you noticed this table, at
which new members of the Middle Temple are sworn
in. The wood came from the cover of the forehatch
of Sir Francis Drake's Golden Hinde. He often ate
and drank in this hall, the old buccaneer. The members of the Middle Temple Inn gave him a great welcome here in 1586, when he returned from the Indies
with looted Spanish gold.

Watson: And the large table over there – is that the high
table for the leading officers of the Inn?

Shakespeare: So it is. It was made from three planks,
each 29 feet long. Queen Elizabeth donated the
wood from an oak tree that grew in the forest of
Windsor, and it was brought here, almost to the
door, on the river. Now, let me tell you about the
first performance of *Twelfth Night*. I played Malvolio, one of my very best comic roles. He wears yellow cross-garters …

Holmes: Mr Shakespeare, we are most obliged to you,
but I'm afraid we really must …

Shakespeare *(interrupts)*: And another thing. Did

zu beneiden. Dann warfen sie Bierkrüge und Hühnerbeine, manchmal noch viel schlimmere Sachen.

Holmes: Diese Ausführungen sind hochinteressant, Mr Shakespeare – und wir fühlen uns geehrt, es von Ihnen, dem großen Barden, zu hören –, aber wir sind gekommen, weil wir Middle Temple Hall in Augenschein nehmen müssen.

Shakespeare *(führt sie in die Aula hinein)*: Dann kommen Sie mit. Schauen Sie auf die wunderschöne doppelte Stichbalkendecke. Es gibt keine herrlichere Kulisse für eine Schauspieltruppe! Sehen Sie diesen Tisch? Dort werden neue Mitglieder des Middle Temple vereidigt. Das Holz stammt von der Abdeckung der vorderen Luke der «Golden Hinde», Sir Francis Drakes Schiff. Er trank und speiste oft in dieser Halle, der alte Freibeuter. Die Juristen des Middle Temple Inn feierten ihn im Jahre 1586, als er aus Westindien mit geplündertem spanischen Gold zurückkehrte.

Watson: Und der mächtige Tisch drüben ist sicher für die hohen Amtsträger des Inn?

Shakespeare: Richtig. Aus drei Brettern gezimmert, jedes Brett 29 Fuß lang. Dafür spendete Königin Elizabeth das Holz – von einer Eiche aus dem Forst von Windsor –, das auf der Themse verschifft wurde, bis fast hierher vor die Tür. Was ich aber erzählen wollte: Bei der Uraufführung von ‹Was ihr wollt› spielte ich Malvolio, eine meiner gelungensten komischen Rollen. Er trägt mit Bändern umwickelte gelbe Strümpfe …

Holmes: Vielen Dank für diese Auskünfte, Mr Shakespeare, aber ich fürchte, wir müssen jetzt …

Shakespeare *(unterbricht ihn)*: Und noch etwas. Wussten Sie,

you know that I set a scene from one of my history plays, *Henry VI*, in the Inner Temple garden? It was to show how the Wars of the Roses began. Richard Plantagenet calls on those who support him to pick a white rose. The Earl of Somerset, for his part, picks a red rose, and that's how the two sides got their emblems. The Temple garden is famous for its roses.

Holmes *(bows his head slightly to the poet)***:** We are going to the Inner Temple now, and we will not fail to admire the garden. Many thanks for your help.

He strides rapidly out of Middle Temple Hall, Watson at his heels. They go back up Middle Temple Lane a short way and turn right into Pump Court. After crossing this court they reach a church on the property of the Inner Temple.

The varied mix of persons who have been members of the Inner Temple includes the poet Geoffrey Chaucer, the the leading proponents of Indian independence Gandhi and Nehru, and a well-known German member of the resistance to Hitler, James, Count von Moltke, who was tried and executed in 1945 following Stauffenberg's attempted assassination of Hitler.
In about 1160 the Order of Knights Templar founded a monastery on the north bank of the Thames and built a round church, modelled on the Church of the Holy Sepulchre in Jerusalem. The Round Church, to which a rectangular chancel was later added, harbours rare effigies of knights from the 13th century. The church sur-

dass ich eine Szene aus einem meiner Königsdramen, ‹Heinrich VI.›, in den Garten des Inner Temple verlegt habe? Es ging um den Anfang der Rosenkriege. Richard Plantagenet bittet alle, die ihn unterstützen, eine weiße Rose zu pflücken. Der Earl of Somerset pflückt seinerseits eine rote Rose, und schon kamen die beiden Parteien zu ihren Symbolen. Der Garten im Temple ist für seine Rosen berühmt.

Holmes *(verneigt sich leicht vor dem Dichter)*: Der Inner Temple ist unser nächstes Ziel. Wir werden nicht versäumen, den Garten zu bewundern. Wir sind Ihnen sehr verbunden.

Er schreitet rasch aus der Middle Temple Hall. Watson eilt hinterher. Sie gehen ein kurzes Stück zurück über die Middle Temple Lane und biegen nach rechts in den Pump Court ein. Diesen Hof durchqueren sie und gelangen zu einer Kirche auf dem Gebiet des Inner Temple.

Zu den ehemaligen Mitgliedern des Inner Temple zählen so unterschiedliche Personen wie der Dichter Geoffrey Chaucer, die führenden Verfechter der Unabhängigkeit Indiens, Gandhi und Nehru, und der deutsche bekannte Widerständler Helmuth James Graf von Moltke, der nach Stauffenbergs Attentat auf Hitler vor Gericht gestellt und 1945 hingerichtet wurde.
Um das Jahr 1160 gründete der Templerorden ein Kloster am nördlichen Themseufer und baute nach dem Vorbild der Grabeskirche in Jerusalem eine runde Kirche. Die Round Church, die später durch einen rechteckigen Kirchenchor im Osten erweitert wurde, birgt Gräber mit Ritterfiguren aus dem 13. Jahr-

vived the bloody suppression of the Knights Templar
in 1312 and became a place of worship for the lawyers
of the Inner Temple. To this day the priest at the church
holds the title once used for the head of the monastery: Master of the Temple.

Following severe damage by incendiary bombs on
the night of 10 May 1941, the Temple Church was restored in the post-war years. To the south of it lies the
historic garden with its lawns and flower beds. Before
the Embankment road was built in the 19th century,
the garden ran down to the river bank. The buildings
to the east of the garden, in King's Bench Walk, date
from the 17th century.

As Holmes and Watson enter the Round Church, a
tall knight steps into their path. Over his armour he is
wearing a white tunic with a red cross.

Holmes: Do we have the honour of meeting a Templar
Knight?

Knight: My name is William Marshal, 1st Earl of Pembroke and Regent of England. If you have come here
with peaceful intentions, you are welcome. If not,
prepare to feel the bite of my sword!

Holmes: We are concerned that someone is plotting to
damage this church. That is why we have come.

William Marshal: Your presence is not needed: I protect
the Temple Church. This place is dear to my heart. Look,
that's my grave, and this effigy represents my eldest son,
and that one over is my third son. Word of my reputation
has surely reached your ears. I was the best and bravest
knight of my time, the only one who ever unhorsed Rich-

hundert. Das Ensemble überlebte die blutige Auflösung des Ordens im Jahr 1312 und wurde zu einem
Gotteshaus der Juristenkörperschaft. Der erste Priester
der Kirche heißt bis heute «Master of the Temple» in
Anlehnung an den Titel des Oberhaupts des ehemaligen Klosters.
Die Temple Church wurde nach schwerer Zerstörung
durch Brandbomben in der Nacht vom 10. Mai 1941
restauriert. Südlich erstreckt sich der historische Garten
mit Rasen und Rosenbeeten. Vor dem Bau der Embankment Road im 19. Jahrhundert, reichte der Garten bis
zum Flussufer. Die Häuser östlich davon im King's
Bench Walk stammen noch aus dem 17. Jahrhundert.

Als Holmes und Watson die Round Curch betreten, stellt sich
ihnen ein hochgewachsener Ritter in den Weg. Über seiner
Rüstung trägt er eine weiße Tunika mit einem roten Kreuz.

Holmes: Haben wir etwa die Ehre, einen Kreuzritter zu treffen?

Ritter: Ich bin William Marshal, erster Earl of Pembroke
und Regent von England. Wenn Sie Gutes im Schilde füh-
ren, sind Sie hier willkommen. Sonst nehmen Sie sich in
Acht!

Holmes: Wir haben Sorge, dass jemand diese Kirche beschädigen möchte. Deshalb sind wir gekommen.

William Marshal: Völlig unnötig – ich beschütze die Temple
Church. Dieser Ort liegt mir sehr am Herzen. Hier sehen
Sie mein Grab, diese Figur stellt meinen ältesten Sohn dar,
und da drüben liegt mein dritter. Mein Ruf dürfte Ihnen
bekannt sein. Ich war der beste und tapferste Ritter meiner Zeit, der Einzige, der jemals Richard Löwenherz aus

ard the Lionheart. When I was a young man, I earned my living by taking part in tournaments in France. They were real battles, with dead and wounded. We took prisoners, and demanded ransom for them. So old King Henry – the second of that name, the father of Richard and John – entrusted me with the task of making sure his other son, young Prince Henry, was never captured. That would have been expensive for the kingdom.

Holmes: Was it the mission of Knights Templar to take part in tournaments?

William Marshal: Of course not! But many years later I went to Jerusalem as a pilgrim and swore there that I would take the cross as a Temple knight. I kept my oath: as I lay dying, the Templars took me into their ranks.

Watson: The leg of your funeral effigy is resting on the figure of a dog. Was that your favourite hound?

William Marshal: The dog is a symbol of loyalty. I always faithfully served Church and Crown, and no man in England was more highly respected than I was. Here in the grounds of the Temple I mediated between King John and the barons. The king confirmed the rights that were recorded in Magna Carta. After John's death I held the office of regent for his son, Henry III, who was a minor. I defeated the boy king's enemies at the Battle of Lincoln – 70 years old then, but I still went into battle and was victorious.

Watson: And you have been protecting this church for almost 700 years?

William Marshal: I'll avert danger from this holy place, come what may – and 100 years after my death, evil

dem Sattel gestoßen hat. Als junger Mann verdiente ich mein Geld in Turnieren in Frankreich. Es waren richtige Schlachten – es gab Tote und Verletzte, wir nahmen Gefangene und erhielten Lösegeld. Mir übertrug der alte König Henry – der zweite mit dem Namen, Vater von Richard und John – die Aufgabe, zu verhindern, dass der junge Prinz Henry in die Hände seiner Feinde fiel. Das hätte das Königreich teuer bezahlen müssen …

Holmes: Hatten Tempelritter den Auftrag, an Turnieren teilzunehmen?

William Marshal: Natürlich nicht! Aber viele Jahre später ging ich als Pilger nach Jerusalem und schwor dort, in den Templerorden einzutreten. Das Gelübde hielt ich – als ich im Sterben lag, nahmen mich die Tempelritter in ihre Reihen auf.

Watson: Auf dem Grab ruht Ihr Bein auf der Figur eines Hundes. War das Ihr Lieblingshund?

William Marshal: Der Hund steht für Treue. Kirche und Krone blieb ich immer treu, und kein Mann in England genoss so hohes Ansehen wie ich. Hier im Tempelbezirk vermittelte ich zwischen König John und den Baronen. Der König bestätigte die Rechte, die in der Magna Carta festgehalten wurden. Nach Johns Tod war ich Regent für seinen minderjährigen Sohn Henry III. und schlug dessen Gegner in der Schlacht von Lincoln nieder – mit 70 Jahren zog ich noch in den Kampf und war siegreich.

Watson: Und seit fast 700 Jahren schützen Sie diese Kirche?

William Marshal: Ich wehre jede Gefahr ab, komme, was wolle – und 100 Jahre nach meinem Tod brach eine

times did come. King Philip of France accused the knights of many terrible crimes. My pious brothers were tortured until they confessed. It was all a pretext: the French king needed money, and the Templar order had great estates and had become rich from lending money. He coerced the pope into abolishing the order. Here in England our possessions eventually fell into the hands of the lawyers. It was an injustice. The Knights Templar were honest servants of God. If one of us committed a crime, we settled the matter ourselves. Come and look at this.

He takes them to the part of the building that connects the Round Church and the chancel, and points to two narrow openings, high in the wall on the north side.

William Marshal: That is the punishment cell. It's only four and a half feet long, so that prisoners could not lie down. When the preceptor of the order in Ireland embezzled money, we locked him up there. It was eight weeks before he starved to death. And I'd be inclined to do the same to that thin-looking man with a black beard who was nosing around yesterday in my church, as if he was trying to hide something. Is that the man you say means to do harm here? He ran away from me and dropped this. Perhaps you know what it is for. Take it – you seem to be trustworthy.

He hands a black fountain pen to Holmes.

Holmes: Thank you! This may help us to track him down.

schlimme Zeit an. Der König von Frankreich bezichtigte den Orden, alle möglichen furchtbaren Untaten begangen zu haben. Meine frommen Brüder wurden gefoltert, bis sie gestanden. Aber das war alles ein Vorwand – der Orden hatte große Ländereien und viel Geld durch Bankgeschäfte. Er zwang den Papst, den Orden aufzulösen. Unser Besitz hier in England kam in der Folge in die Hände der Juristen. Ein himmelschreiendes Unrecht! Die Tempelritter waren aufrichtige Diener Gottes. Wir sorgten selber für Ordnung, wenn einer von uns eine Straftat beging. Schauen Sie hier!

Er führt sie in einen anderen Teil der Kirche und zeigt auf zwei schmale Fenster in Höhe der ersten Etage auf der Nordseite zwischen der Runde und dem Chor.

William Marshal: Das ist die Strafzelle. Sie ist nur viereinhalb Fuß lang, sodass kein Gefangener sich hinlegen konnte. Als der Präzeptor des Ordens in Irland Gelder veruntreute, sperrten wir ihn dort ein, bis er nach acht Wochen verhungerte. Mit dem hageren, schwarzbärtigen Mann, der sich gestern in der Kirche herumtrieb und wohl ein Versteck suchte, wäre ich gerne genauso verfahren. Er flüchtete vor mir und ließ das hier fallen. Vielleicht wissen Sie, was es ist. Nehmen Sie es – Sie scheinen mir vertrauenswürdig zu sein.

Er überreicht Holmes einen schwarzen Füllfederhalter.

Holmes: Tausend Dank! Das wird uns helfen, seine Spur aufzunehmen.

11.

A Literary Pub
(Ye Olde Cheshire Cheese)

Eine Literatenkneipe
(Ye Olde Cheshire Cheese)

... up a covered way, into a tavern ... where Charles
Darnay was soon recruiting his strength with
a good plain dinner and good wine.

From *A Tale of Two Cities*, Charles Dickens

From the Temple Church Holmes and Watson walk
back up to Fleet Street, where they turn right and head
east. After about 300 metres, a little beyond Whitefriars
Street, they look across to no. 145 Fleet Street on the
opposite side of the road. It is an inconspicuous building with a brown brick façade. A sign declares it to be
Ye Olde Cheshire Cheese.

> A tavern occupied this site as long ago as the 16th
> century. In its present form the Cheshire Cheese was
> built in 1667, a year after the Great Fire of London, but
> the cellars are older and probably belonged to a Car-
> melite monastery that was founded here in the 13th
> century. The pub's name is a reminder that Chesh-
> ire cheese was the most popular English cheese 200
> years ago. Now crumbly and fresh-tasting, in those
> days it was matured longer to make it hard for the
> journey by sea from Chester to London. As a nutri-
> tious product that could be stored for months, it was
> once part of the supplies on all Royal Navy ships.

Holmes and Watson cross Fleet Street and enter the
pub from the door in Wine Office Court, a passage next
to the Cheshire Cheese. Inside they take a brief look at
the dining room on the left, then go into the taproom

Einen überdachten Gang hinauf, in eine Taverne hinein …
wo Charles Darnay mit guter, einfacher Kost und
gutem Wein bald wieder zu Kräften kam.

Aus ‹Eine Geschichte aus zwei Städten›, Charles Dickens

Von der Temple Church kehren Holmes und Watson zur Fleet
Street zurück und gehen rechts Richtung Osten. Nach etwa
300 Metern, etwas oberhalb von der Whitefriars Street, sehen
sie Nr. 145 Fleet Street auf der gegenüberliegenden Straßen-
seite. Es ist ein unscheinbares Haus aus braunem Backstein.
Davor hängt ein Kneipenschild: Ye Olde Cheshire Cheese.

An dieser Stelle stand bereits im 16. Jahrhundert eine
Kneipe. Der Pub in seiner heutigen Form wurde 1667,
ein Jahr nach dem Großen Brand von London, gebaut,
doch die Keller sind älter und gehörten vermutlich zu
einem Karmeliterkloster, das im 13. Jahrhundert hier
gegründet wurde. Der Name bezieht sich auf die vor
200 Jahren beliebteste Käsesorte des Landes. Cheshire
Cheese, heute krümelig und frisch im Geschmack,
musste er, um hart zu werden, länger reifen, damit er
die Reise auf dem Seeweg von der Grafschaft Cheshire
im Nordwesten des Landes nach London überstehen
konnte. Früher gehörte das haltbare Nahrungsmittel zu
den Vorräten aller Schiffe der königlichen Marine.

Holmes und Watson überqueren die Fleet Street und gehen
in den Wine Office Court, eine enge Gasse neben dem Haus,
wo sich der Eingang zur Kneipe befindet. Sie gehen hinein,
schauen kurz nach links in den Speiseraum und begeben

on the right, greeting the landlord behind the bar with a nod. Dark wood panelling covers the walls and ceiling of the room. Between the window, which admits little light from the narrow passage outside, and the hearth, where no fire has been laid on this warm June evening, stand a few plain tables

The solitary guest, a man in his late thirties with short dark hair and a luxuriant walrus moustache, is sitting at a corner table. He is dressed in a three-piece tweed suit. He is chewing the end of a fountain pen, and has a furrowed brow. Even in the dim light it is obvious that the hand-written sheet of paper in front of him is covered with blots of ink, numerous crossings-out, and additions scrawled between the lines and in the margins. He seems completely immersed in his work and does not look up when Holmes and Watson enter. Holmes walks over to the table, glances briefly at the paper and speaks to the writer.

Holmes: Dr Conan Doyle, good evening. Are you working on a new historical novel?

Conan Doyle: Oh, Holmes! Aaaaah ... I wasn't expecting to see you here. And Dr Watson. Well, good evening to you, too. Errrrrm ...

The author covers part of the manuscript with the sleeve of his jacket.

Holmes: It's extremely difficult to remove ink from tweed cloth – a circumstance that has proved useful to me more than once in solving a case. However, there is absolutely no reason why you should feel embarrassed. I perfectly understand that you might want a change from recording my cases.

sich dann in die Stube mit Bierausschank rechter Hand und nicken dem Wirt hinter dem Tresen zu. Dunkles Holz verkleidet die Wände und Decke des Raums. Einige einfache Tische stehen zwischen dem Fenster, das wenig Licht von draußen hereinlässt, und einem Kamin. An diesem warmen Juniabend brennt dort kein Feuer.

Der einzige Gast in der Stube sitzt an einem Tisch in der Ecke. Der Mann trägt einen dreiteiligen Tweedanzug, ist vielleicht Ende 30, hat kurze dunkle Haare und einen üppigen Schnauzbart mit Spitzen. Er kaut an einem Füllerfederhalter und runzelt die Stirn. Auch im schwachen Licht fällt auf, dass das Blatt vor ihm zahlreiche Tintenkleckse, durchgestrichene Passagen und Änderungen zwischen den Zeilen und am Rand aufweist. Er scheint ganz in seine Arbeit vertieft und schaut nicht auf. Holmes geht zu dem Tisch hinüber, wirft einen Blick auf das Blatt und spricht den Schreibenden an.

Holmes: Dr. Conan Doyle, guten Abend. Arbeiten Sie an einem neuen historischen Roman?

Conan Doyle: Oh, Holmes! Aaaaah … Sie habe ich hier nicht erwartet. Und Dr. Watson. Guten Abend. Äähm …

Der Autor deckt einen Teil seines Manuskripts mit dem Ärmel ab.

Holmes: Es ist äußerst schwierig, Tinte von Tweedstoff zu entfernen – eine Tatsache, die mir mehr als einmal bei der Lösung eines Falls genutzt hat. Aber es besteht kein Grund zur Verlegenheit. Ich verstehe es vollkommen, wenn Sie eine Abwechslung vom Verfassen meiner Kriminalfälle suchen.

Conan Doyle: You grasped it straight away, Holmes. I'd like to broaden my repertoire as an author, and try something creative, so I'm working on a naval subject, a novel set in the time of the Napoleonic wars.

Holmes: I suppose you were hoping to take inspiration from the literary associations of this tavern. However, if the muse should prove to be reluctant, Dr Watson has permission to inform you of my recent investigations – as soon as they have come to a successful conclusion, of course, and are ready for publication.

Watson: If I may give some advice as one physician to another: the light in here is extremely gloomy for the purpose of writing. You're an ophthalmologist yourself, I believe …

Conan Doyle: My medical practice had no success, I'm afraid. And yes, you're right, the landlord here isn't generous with candles and lamps, but in these surroundings, where Dr Johnson, Charles Dickens and Lord Tennyson entertained their friends, a writer can't help feeling at home. Besides, the lamb chops are delicious.

Holmes: May I congratulate you on the memoirs that you published last year about some of my more interesting cases? You are certainly a conscientious chronicler, and the book deserved its success. It was very convenient to me that the last story ended with my apparent death. I was able to disappear for a while on my travels, and carry on my work covertly after returning.

Conan Doyle: My readers were extremely disappointed to think there would be no more Sherlock Holmes adventures.

Holmes: I should have thought that sincere regret and

Conan Doyle: Sie haben es sofort erfasst, Holmes. Ich möchte meinen Ruf als Schriftsteller auf eine breitere Basis stellen, mich an etwas Neuem versuchen, und arbeite an einer Geschichte, die zur Zeit der Kriege gegen Napoleon spielt.

Holmes: Ich vermute, dass Sie sich von den literarischen Assoziationen dieser Taverne Inspiration erhoffen. Wenn diese ausbleiben sollte, hat Dr. Watson die Erlaubnis, Sie über meine neuen Ermittlungen in Kenntnis zu setzen – sobald diese abgeschlossen und für eine Veröffentlichung reif sind, versteht sich.

Watson: Wenn ich Ihnen einen Ratschlag geben darf, von einem Mediziner zum anderen: Das Licht hier drinnen ist zu schwach, um dabei zu schreiben. Sie sind ja selbst Augenarzt …

Conan Doyle: Meine Arztpraxis war leider nicht von Erfolg gekrönt. Aber ja, Sie haben recht. Der Wirt geizt mit Kerzen und Lampen. Trotzdem – an dem Ort, an dem Dr. Johnson, Charles Dickens und Lord Tennyson mit ihren Freunden verkehrten, fühlt man sich als Schreiberling wohl. Außerdem sind die Lammkoteletts hier köstlich.

Holmes: Darf ich zu den Memoiren gratulieren, die Sie letztes Jahr über einige meiner interessantesten Fälle veröffentlichten? Sie sind wirklich ein gewissenhafter Chronist, und das Buch war ein verdienter Erfolg. Es kam mir gelegen, dass die letzte Geschichte mit meinem angeblichen Tod endete. So konnte ich eine Weile auf Reisen gehen und nach meiner Rückkehr im Verborgenen arbeiten.

Conan Doyle: Meine Leser waren enttäuscht bei der Vorstellung, dass es keine weiteren Abenteuer von Sherlock Holmes geben würde.

Holmes: Wären aufrichtige Anteilnahme und Trauer über

mourning at my demise were more appropriate than disappointment at losing a source of entertainment. After all, I'm not a fictional character. Never mind – word has now got about that I survived the fight with Professor Moriarty at the Reichenbach Falls, and it's known that I'm back in London. So you are free to record the true version of events when your efforts with the historical novel have ended. By the way, I noticed something in your manuscript. As you know, I can read even spidery handwriting upside down. You've written that Lord Nelson had no right eye. That's not correct – he didn't lose the eye, only the sight of the right eye. I wonder if you could have healed him?

Conan Doyle looks confused, refers to his manuscript and shakes his head in irritation.

Holmes: We have work to do here, so we'll leave you in peace. Goodbye!

Ye Olde Cheshire Cheese does indeed have distinguished literary connections. The author of the first dictionary of the English language, Dr Samuel Johnson, lived close by, and his chair is on display in the pub although there is no written record of his presence. In the 19th century Charles Dickens, Mark Twain and the poet laureate Lord Tennyson, as well as Sir Arthur Conan Doyle at a later date, dined and drank here. Dickens referred to the pub, without mentioning its name, in *A Tale of Two Cities* in a scene when Charles Darnay, who has just been acquitted of high treason, is taken there for a meal.

meinen Tod nicht angemessener gewesen als Enttäuschung darüber, eine Quelle der Unterhaltung zu verlieren? Ich bin schließlich kein fiktiver Charakter. Aber gut! Es hat sich mittlerweile herumgesprochen, dass ich den Kampf mit Professor Moriarty am Reichenbachfall überlebt habe und wieder in London bin. Sie können also den wahren Sachverhalt schreiben, wenn Ihre Bemühungen mit dem historischen Roman beendet sind. Übrigens, mir fällt in Ihrem Text etwas auf – Sie wissen ja, ich kann eine krakelige Schrift auch kopfüber lesen. Sie haben geschrieben, dass Lord Nelson das rechte Auge fehlte. So war es nicht. Er behielt das Auge, verlor aber sein Sehvermögen. Hätten Sie ihn erfolgreich behandeln können?

Conan Doyle blickt verwirrt, wendet sich wieder seinem Manuskript zu und schüttelt ärgerlich den Kopf …

Holmes: Wir haben noch einiges zu tun, also lassen wir Sie nun in Ruhe. Auf Wiedersehen!

Ye Olde Cheshire Cheese hat tatsächlich beste Verbindungen zu der Welt der Literatur. Der Verfasser des ersten Wörterbuches der englischen Sprache, Dr. Samuel Johnson, wohnte in der Nachbarschaft – sein Stuhl wird im Pub gezeigt, obwohl es nicht verbürgt ist, dass er je da war. Im 19. Jahrhundert waren Charles Dickens, Mark Twain, der Hofdichter Lord Tennyson – und später Sir Arthur Conan Doyle – oft hier zu Gast. Dickens erwähnt die Kneipe – allerdings nicht namentlich – im Roman ‹Eine Geschichte aus zwei Städten›, als der des Hochverrats angeklagte Charles Darnay nach seinem Freispruch dorthin geführt wird.

Holmes *(goes over to the bar and speaks to the landlord)*: We're looking for a red-haired man named Jim Barnes. Is he here?

Landlord *(nudges a boy who is standing next to him, and aims a look towards the entrance hall)*: Jim's found a job, and I don't see him as much as I used to. If he turns up again, I'll say that two gentlemen were looking for him. Are you plain-clothes policemen?

The boy has left the taproom and Holmes hears the sound of him running down the stairs that lead from the hall to the cellar. Holmes follows, but with his tall frame has to duck under a low sill and descend the steep steps carefully. When he arrives at the bottom, the boy is out of sight. A few men in working clothes look up from their ale and stare at the detective. In a corner Holmes notices a high-backed wooden bench behind an empty table. The tankard on the table is full to the brim, and next to it wax is dripping from a candle-holder that has been knocked over. Holmes hurries into a second room, just in time to see that a door beneath a pointed arch in the low, brick-vaulted ceiling is being closed from the other side. He hears someone bolting the door, then footsteps becoming more distant. The landlord's boy is standing next to the door.

Holmes *(holds out a shilling)*: I'm sure you can tell me where Jim Barnes works.

Boy: In the engine room at the new bridge. He's a stoker.

Holmes: Did he meet anyone here yesterday? A large thin man with a hooked nose and a bushy beard.

Holmes *(geht zum Tresen und spricht den Wirt an)*: Wir suchen einen rothaarigen Mann namens Jim Barnes. Ist er hier?

Wirt *(stupst einen Jungen neben ihm an und wirft einen Blick in den Flur)*: Jim hat Arbeit gefunden, seitdem sehe ich ihn nicht mehr so oft. Wenn er auftaucht, sage ich, dass zwei Herren ihn suchen. Sind Sie Polizisten in Zivil?

Der Junge hat den Schankraum verlassen. Holmes hört, dass er vom Flur aus die Stufen zum Keller hinunterrennt, und folgt ihm. Auf der steilen, engen Treppe muss der hochgewachsene Detektiv den Kopf einziehen und vorsichtig hinuntergehen. Unten angekommen, sieht er den Jungen nicht mehr. Einige Männer in Arbeitskleidung blicken von ihrem Bier auf und starren ihn an. In einer Ecke bemerkt Holmes eine Holzbank mit hoher Rückenlehne. Der Tisch davor ist unbesetzt, der Bierkrug darauf aber voll. Von einem umgestürzten Kerzenständer tropft heißes Wachs auf den Tisch. Holmes eilt in einen zweiten Raum, wo eine Tür unter einem spitzen Bogen im Backsteingewölbe gerade von außen geschlossen wird. Er hört, wie jemand sie verriegelt, dann sich entfernende Fußtritte. Neben der Tür steht der Junge.

Holmes *(hält ihm einen Schilling entgegen)*: Du weißt sicher, wo Jim Barnes arbeitet?

Junge: Im Maschinenraum der neuen Brücke. Er ist Heizer.

Holmes: Hat er sich gestern mit jemandem hier getroffen? Ein großer, schlanker Mann mit Hakennase und einem buschigen Bart.

Boy: Yes, that's what the man looked like. He had horrible, piercing eyes.

The boy bites the shilling, turns away and disappears
up the stairs.

Holmes *(to Watson, who arrives out of breath)*:
Barnes has escaped, but now we know where to find
him. It's time to examine the fountain pen that the
other man left behind in the Temple Church.

Holmes takes a seat and removes the pen, a sheet of
paper and his magnifying glass from a pocket. He writes
a few words with the pen, then scrutinises the nib and
the paper closely.

Holmes: Even in this dim cellar I can see beyond doubt
that this was the pen and the ink that the blackmailer
used to write to the prime minister. The way the nib
has worn down tells me he is right-handed and has
long arms. We have clear confirmation that the mysterious thin man is the criminal behind the awful threat.
Watson: Well, if we know where to look for the red-
head Jim Barnes, and can expect to find the blackmailer with him, then that leaves us time to eat a
lamb chop before we press on with the hunt.
Holmes: Quite right, Watson. It's already seven o'clock,
and we should refresh ourselves and gather strength
for what lies ahead. Our opponent has been careless,
and he certainly lacks the cunning and ability of my
old adversary Moriarty, but I believe we'll face danger
before the evening is out.

Junge: Ja, so sah der Mann aus. Er hatte furchtbare, bohrende Augen.

Prüfend beißt der Junge auf die Münze, dreht sich um und verschwindet über die Treppe.

Holmes *(zu Watson, der außer Atem angekommen ist)*: Barnes ist entkommen, aber wir wissen jetzt, wo wir ihn finden. Ich werde nun diesen Füllfederhalter untersuchen, den der andere Mann in der Temple Church fallen ließ.

Holmes setzt sich, holt den Füllfederhalter, ein Blatt Papier und eine Lupe aus seiner Jackentasche. Nachdem er einige Worte mit dem Füller geschrieben hat, begutachtet er Papier und Feder sorgfältig.

Holmes: Auch in diesem schummrigen Keller ist der Fall klar. Mit dieser Feder und Tinte schrieb der Erpresser an den Premierminister. Die Abnutzung der Feder sagt mir, dass er ein Rechtshänder ist und lange Arme hat. Hier haben wir also die Bestätigung, dass der dünne Unbekannte hinter der furchtbaren Drohung steckt.

Watson: Wenn wir wissen, wo wir den rothaarigen Jim Barnes suchen müssen, finden wir den Erpresser hoffentlich mit ihm zusammen. Dann bleibt uns Zeit, hier ein Lammkotelett zu verspeisen, bevor wir uns weiter auf die Suche begeben.

Holmes: Ganz recht, Watson. Es ist bereits 19 Uhr, und für das, was uns bevorsteht, sollten wir uns jetzt stärken. Unser Gegner war unvorsichtig und hat nicht das Kaliber meines alten Widersachers Moriarty, aber bevor der Tag vorbei ist, begeben wir uns sicher in Gefahr.

12.

The Architect and his Dome
(St Paul's Cathedral)

Der Architekt und seine Kuppel
(St Paul's Cathedral)

If you require a monument, look around you.
Epitaph in St Paul's Cathedral for Sir Christopher Wren

St Paul's Cathedral stands on a hill which has been crowned by a church for 1400 years. Its dome radiates a majestic calm over the bustle and noise of the City of London. In 1666 the Great Fire destroyed the previous building, Old St Paul's. Christopher Wren was then commissioned to design and oversee the construction of a new cathedral, which was completed in 1711 after 36 years of work. Today it is a national icon, and it has long been the stage for great events. Queen Victoria celebrated her diamond jubilee in St Paul's in 1897; in 1981 Prince Charles and Lady Diana Spencer married there. The great British military commanders of the Napoleonic Wars, Admiral Nelson and the Duke of Wellington, as well as empire-builders of the 19th century such as General Gordon and Lord Kitchener, are buried in the chapels and crypt. When German bombs rained down on London in 1940 and 1941, St Paul's became a powerful symbol of the will to fight. During one night of particularly heavy raids, as fires threatened to engulf the whole area around the cathedral, Churchill gave the order that St Paul's should be saved at all costs, as its dome, rising amid flames, smoke and the searchlights that probed the night sky, represented defiance in the face of a terrible threat.

Wenn du ein Denkmal suchst, schaue dich um.

Epitaph in der St. Paul's Cathedral für Sir Christopher Wren

Mit ihrer hohen Kuppel krönt die Kathedrale eine Erhebung, die seit 1400 Jahren Standort einer Kirche ist, und strahlt über dem lauten Trubel der City of London eine souveräne Ruhe aus. 1666 zerstörte der Große Brand von London die Vorgängerkirche Old St Paul's. Christopher Wren erhielt den Auftrag, eine neue Kathedrale zu planen und die Bauarbeiten zu leiten. Nach 36 Jahren Bauzeit wurde sie im Jahr 1711 vollendet und hat heute den Status eines Nationalheiligtums. St Paul's ist seit langer Zeit Schauplatz großer Feierlichkeiten: Hier feierte Königin Victoria 1897 ihr 60. Thronjubiläum, heirateten 1981 Prinz Charles und Lady Diana Spencer. Die größten britischen Militärhelden der Napoleonischen Kriege, Admiral Nelson und der Duke of Wellington, sowie Begründer der britischen Imperialmacht im 19. Jahrhundert, wie General Gordon und Lord Kitchener, wurden in der Kapelle und Krypta bestattet.

Während der deutschen Bombenangriffe auf London von 1940 bis 1941 wurde St Paul's zu einem wichtigen Symbol des Kampfeswillen. Als in einer Nacht mit besonders schlimmen Angriffen ein Großbrand drohte, diesen Stadtteil um die Kathedrale in Schutt und Asche zu verwandeln, gab Churchill den Befehl, um jeden Preis St Paul's zu retten, denn inmitten der Flammen und Rauchschwaden, von den Scheinwerferstrahlen des Luftschutzes umgeben, verkörperte die Kuppel den ungebrochenen Willen, der schrecklichen Bedrohung Widerstand zu leisten.

Watson and Holmes walk east along Fleet Street to Ludgate Circus, where Ludgate Street leads up to St Paul's Cathedral. They reach the statue of Queen Anne that stands close to the west towers of the cathedral.

Watson: The cab driver Mays said he followed our suspect this far, and last saw him entering the cathedral. Well, Holmes, do you expect to meet a ghost from the past here, too?

Holmes: I hope so. I would enjoy a talk with the architect. Wren had a brilliant mind. He was a mathematician and professor of astronomy. You know my principles, Watson: I aim to solve the most difficult cases through the power of logical reasoning and scientific analysis. Wren was a man of science, and the study of physics sparked off his interest in architecture. He conceived original solutions to problems of spanning space and bearing loads. He researched fundamental answers to the questions that interested him – a man after my own heart! And if I'm not mistaken, here he comes.

Holmes gestures to a figure wearing a brown wig that falls to his shoulders in thick locks. He has a long, pointed nose and a questioning look in his clear eyes.

Wren: I was expecting you, gentlemen. Word reached me that you appreciated St Paul's Church in Covent Garden, a masterpiece by my great predecessor Inigo Jones. Now you can survey St Paul's Cathedral and make up your mind whether I surpassed Jones's

Watson und Holmes laufen auf der Fleet Street Richtung Osten zum Ludgate Circus, wo die Ludgate Street zu St Paul's Cathedral hinaufführt. Sie nähern sich der Statue der Königin Anne nahe den Westtürmen der Kathedrale.

Watson: Der Droschkenfahrer Mays sagte, dass er dem Verdächtigen bis hierhin gefolgt sei und zuletzt gesehen habe, wie er die Kathedrale betrat. Was meinen Sie, Holmes, treffen wir wieder einen Geist aus alten Zeiten?

Holmes: Ich hoffe es. Ich würde mich gern mit dem Architekten unterhalten. Wren war ein brillanter Kopf, Mathematiker und Professor der Astronomie. Sie kennen meine Prinzipien, Watson: Mein Anspruch ist es, die schwierigsten Fälle durch logische Schlussfolgerungen und wissenschaftliche Methoden zu lösen. Wren war ein Mann der Wissenschaft, der über sein Studium der Physik an die Architektur kam. Er konzipierte originelle Lösungen für Probleme der Statik und Traglast. Er suchte grundlegende Antworten auf Fragen, die ihn interessierten – ein Mann ganz nach meinem Geschmack! Und wenn mich nicht alles täuscht, kommt er hier schon.

Die Figur, auf die Holmes zeigt, trägt eine lange braune Perücke, deren üppige Locken bis auf seine Schultern herunterfallen. Er hat eine lange, spitze Nase und einen fragenden Blick in seinen klaren Augen.

Wren: Ich habe Sie erwartet, meine Herren. Die Nachricht erreichte mich, dass Sie die Kirche St Paul's in Covent Garden, das Werk meines großen Vorgängers Inigo Jones, mit Freude betrachtet haben. Jetzt können Sie sich an der Kathedrale St Paul's ein Urteil darüber bilden, ob ich Jones'

work. Yes, Nell Gwyn told me she had shown you the church. She and I are good friends. We both served the same king, Charles II – in different positions, admittedly.

Watson: Is it true that you were responsible for building more than 50 churches in London? They say you practically rebuilt the City of London after the Great Fire.

Wren: I would like to have done so, but they didn't let me. Two thirds of the City of London was a smouldering field of rubble. 13,000 houses and 87 churches were destroyed. It was a opportunity that will never come again to start from scratch and reconstruct this higgledy-piggledy old city according to a rational plan. I seized the moment, and presented my scheme to the king only nine days after the outbreak of the fire. I showed him a design with fine squares, like the ones in Paris, and broad avenues with prospects of imposing architecture, just as in Rome. It would have been a spacious, generously planned capital city, radiant with light and beauty, a city to compare with anything else on earth.

Watson: And what happened?

Wren: It's true that I was the architect of 50 churches. But the grand plan was a different matter. The people of London insisted on holding on to their old plots of land, all those tiny holdings and crooked alleyways that made up the city. They wanted new houses as quickly as possible in exactly the same place as before, so they could carry on making money. It was the usual mean-spirited mentality of merchants and shopkeepers. They lacked the patience and imagina-

Werk übertroffen habe. Ja, Nell Gwyn hat mir erzählt, dass sie Ihnen die Kirche gezeigt hat. Sie und ich sind gute Freunde – wir dienten schließlich demselben König, Charles II., allerdings in unterschiedlichen Ämtern.

Watson: Stimmt es, dass Sie für den Bau von über 50 Londoner Kirchen zuständig waren? Man sagt auch, Sie hätten die City of London nach dem Großen Brand gewissermaßen neu geschaffen.

Wren: Ich hätte es gerne getan, man ließ mich nur nicht. Zwei Drittel der Fläche der City of London waren ein schwelendes Ruinenfeld. 13 000 Häuser und 87 Kirchen zerstört! Das war eine einmalige Chance, einen echten Neubeginn zu wagen und diese unüberschaubare alte Stadt nach einem rationalen Schema neu zu errichten. Ich ergriff sie beim Schopf und präsentierte dem König schon neun Tage nach dem Ausbruch der Feuersbrunst meinen Plan – mit stattlichen Plätzen wie in Paris, mit breiten Prachtstraßen, mit Perspektiven auf edle Bauwerke wie in Rom. Es wäre eine großzügige, von Licht und Schönheit erfüllte Hauptstadt gewesen, die mit keiner anderen der Welt den Vergleich gescheut hätte.

Watson: Und was passierte?

Wren: Dass ich der Architekt von 50 Kirchen bin, stimmt ja. Aber der Gesamtplan steht auf einem anderen Blatt. Die Bewohner dieser Stadt hingen an ihren alten Grundstücken, an den mickrigen Parzellen und verwinkelten Gassen. Alle wollten sofort ein neues Haus am selben Platz haben, um schnellstens wieder Geld zu verdienen. Die typische knauserige Mentalität von Kaufleuten und Ladenbesitzern. Ihnen mangelte es an Geduld und Vorstellungskraft, etwas Besseres zu kreieren. Man ver-

tion to create something better. There was even an attempt to repair the old cathedral. Luckily that was not possible, as it was completely ruined.

Watson: And so you designed this magnificent cathedral!

Wren: It wasn't as simple as that. The cathedral clergy rejected my first draft. They said it was too foreign-looking. My second version had the ground plan of a Greek cross – that's a cross with four arms of equal length, and a central part that can be capped with a dome. The philistines! They thought the second design too was an affront to English traditions, and too expensive besides. The third version was a dubious compromise – I admit as much myself. They wanted an old-fashioned steeple, and I was determined to have a dome, so I did a dome with a steeple on top. A strange hybrid. And I gave them an elongated ground plan, like in ancient English cathedrals, and that kept my critics quiet. Then King Charles gave me authority to make changes if I saw fit. That gave me all the leeway I needed, and I used it to the full: later I left off the steeple, and the result has vindicated me.

Holmes: Who paid for the building? Everyone knows that King Charles led an extravagant life. I suppose he was always short of money, and in no position to pay for a cathedral.

Wren: A new tax was levied – not only for St Paul's, but also for the other churches that had to be rebuilt. It was a penny for every ton of coal that was landed in the Port of London. Later there were controversies about the costs of the cathedral, and the tax was doubled. After some 60 years, all the churches were

suchte sogar, die alte Kathedrale zu reparieren. Zum Glück war das nicht möglich, da sie komplett zerstört war.

Watson: Und dann planten Sie dieses umwerfende Bauwerk!

Wren: So einfach war das nicht. Den ersten Entwurf lehnte der Klerus als «zu ausländisch» ab. Mein zweiter Entwurf hatte die Form eines griechischen Kreuzes, also ein Mittelteil mit vier gleich langen Armen, das mit einer Kuppel überdacht werden kann. Auch das empfanden die Banausen als Verstoß gegen die englische Tradition, und außerdem zu teuer. Die dritte Version war ein fauler Kompromiss – das gebe ich selber zu. Sie wollten einen altmodischen Spitzturm, und ich war entschlossen, eine Kuppel zu bauen, und so entwarf ich eine merkwürdige Kombination aus Kuppel und Spitzturm. Und ich plante einen lang gezogenen Grundriss wie bei alten englischen Kathedralen. Damit habe ich meine Kritiker ruhig gestellt. Dann gab König Charles mir die Erlaubnis, Änderungen vorzunehmen, wenn ich sie für notwendig hielt. Einen Freibrief also, den ich voll ausnutzte: den Spitzturm habe ich weggelassen, und das Ergebnis rechtfertigt meine Entscheidung.

Holmes: Wer finanzierte das Gebäude? Jeder weiß, dass König Charles ein extravaganter Lebemann war. Vermutlich war er immer in Geldnöten und konnte nicht für die Kathedrale aufkommen.

Wren: Es gab eine neue Steuer – nicht nur für St Paul's, sondern auch für die anderen Kirchen, die wiederaufgebaut werden mussten. Einen Penny für jede Tonne Kohle, die an den Londoner Hafen geliefert wurde. Dann gab es einen Krach über die Kosten der Kathedrale, und die Steuer wurde verdoppelt. Nach etwa 60 Jahren waren alle Kirchen

finished. But Mr Holmes, do you know when the tax was abolished? Only in 1889. Up to six years ago, you and everyone else had to pay more to heat your rooms, and this cathedral is one of the reasons. So, in recompense, please come inside and admire it.

The architect leads Holmes and Watson into the cathedral. They walk from the west doors through the nave and come to a stop beneath the dome.

Wren: I would like to have seen the dome decorated with mosaics, but the costs were too high and it would have taken many years. So Sir James Thornhill was given the task of painting it. He depicted scenes from the life of St Paul – but they are not at all colourful, and turned out rather dark. However, Mr Holmes, your contemporaries are now making good what we failed to do in my time. The mosaics below the dome, between the arches, are new. And now come into the choir with me. Can you see the work that's going on up there? The vault is being decorated with mosaics. Better late than never! You see, I had to fight against ignorance and shortage of money, but sometimes I was successful. To beautify the building I searched for the best exponents of every craft. Look at these wonderful wrought-iron gates. They were made by Monsieur Jean Tijou. The wood carvings on the choir stalls are by Grinling Gibbons, a great master of his art!

Holmes: Allow me to ask about the construction of the dome. Could it be damaged in such a way as to cause a collapse?

Wren: That would be extremely difficult. A huge quantity

fertig – aber was glauben Sie, Mr Holmes, wann die Steuer abgeschafft wurde? Erst im Jahre 1889. Das heißt, bis vor sechs Jahren hatten auch Sie unter anderem wegen dieser Kathedrale höhere Heizkosten. Kommen Sie bitte hinein, und bestaunen Sie die Kirche als Entschädigung!

Der Architekt führt Holmes und Watson in die Kathedrale. Von den Türen auf der Westseite gehen sie durch das Hauptschiff und bleiben unter der Kuppel stehen.

Wren: Ich hätte die Kuppel gern mit Mosaiken geschmückt, aber das war zu teuer und hätte Jahre gedauert. Der Maler Sir James Thornhill erhielt dann den Auftrag. Er malte Szenen aus dem Leben des Heiligen Paulus – aber sie sind leider etwas eintönig und eher düster geraten. Aber was uns zu meinen Lebzeiten nicht gelungen ist, wird jetzt von Ihren Zeitgenossen wieder gerichtet, Mr Holmes. Diese Mosaiken zwischen den Bögen unter der Kuppel sind ganz neu – und kommen Sie mit in den Chor. Sehen Sie, dass dort oben gearbeitet wird? Das Gewölbe wird mit Mosaiken geschmückt. Endlich! Wissen Sie, ich musste gegen Ignoranz und Geldnot ankämpfen, aber manchmal war ich erfolgreich. Ich suchte die besten Vertreter jedes Handwerks, um dieses Bauwerk so schön zu gestalten. Schauen Sie auf die wunderbaren Tore aus Schmiedeeisen: von Monsieur Jean Tijou. Und die Holzschnitzereien am Chorgestühl: von Grinling Gibbons, ein wahrer Meister seines Fachs!

Holmes: Erlauben Sie mir, nach der Kuppelkonstruktion zu fragen. Könnte man sie zum Einsturz bringen?

Wren: Schwerlich! Eine große Menge Sprengstoff wäre

of explosives would be required. I am especially proud of the dome. It's in three parts. From here you can only see the innermost dome. The one that's visible from outside is a separate structure, and much higher. That was necessary to make the proportions look right. There is a great deal of space between the inner and outer domes, and I used it to insert a cone-shaped construction which supports the outer dome from within and bears the weight of what lies above: the tower and lantern with the golden ball and the cross. It's a conception that works equally well in structural and aesthetic terms.

Watson: It's known far and wide as a great achievement, and all the praise is deserved!

Wren: Thank you – but in my lifetime I was rewarded with animosity. A building commission supervised the work. They kept back half of my salary until the cathedral had been completed, because they thought it was progressing too slowly. When it really was finished – that was in 1711, and I was an old man – times had changed. Charles II was long dead. His brother James II, who succeeded him, fled into exile. Queen Anne, the last monarch of the House of Stuart, had no surviving children, and a German prince from Hanover had been chosen to rule the land. The days when England had good relations to Catholic kingdoms on the continent were over, and this wonderful style of architecture, which I encountered in Rome and France, and took inspiration from, was considered to be foreign, contrary to the spirit of England, and unsuitable for a Protestant country.

Holmes: Despite all of that, your memory was honoured.

notwendig. Auf die Kuppel bin ich besonders stolz. Sie besteht aus drei Teilen. Von hier sehen Sie nur die Innenkuppel. Die von außen sichtbare Kuppel ist eine separate Konstruktion und viel höher, damit die Proportionen stimmen. Zwischen den beiden gibt es enorm viel Raum. Dort baute ich einen hohen Kegel, der die äußere Kuppel von innen stützt und die Last darüber trägt: das oberste Türmchen und die Laterne mit der vergoldeten Kugel und dem Kreuz. Die Statik und die Ästhetik dieses Entwurfs stimmen gleichermaßen.

Watson: Es ist bekanntermaßen eine große Errungenschaft, und Sie verdienen den Ruhm und das Lob!

Wren: Vielen Dank – ich wurde aber zeit meines Lebens mit Anfeindungen belohnt. Eine Baukommission überwachte die Arbeiten. Sie behielten die Hälfte meines Gehalts ein, bis die Kathedrale fertig war, weil es den Herren zu langsam ging. Als es so weit war – wir schrieben das Jahr 1711, ich war ein alter Mann –, hatten sich die Zeiten geändert. König Charles II. war längst tot, sein Bruder König James II. ins Exil geflüchtet. Königin Anne, die Letzte aus dem Hause Stuart, hatte keine Nachkommen, und die Thronfolge war zugunsten eines deutschen Prinzen aus Hannover geregelt. Die Zeit von Englands guten Beziehungen zu den katholischen Königreichen in Europa war vorbei, und diese herrliche Architektur, für die ich in Rom und Frankreich Inspiration holte, galt als kontinental, dem englischen Gemüt widersprechend und unangemessen für ein protestantisches Land.

Holmes: Sie wurden trotzdem geehrt. Das Epitaph im Boden

The epitaph here in the floor is famous: "If you require a monument, look around you."

Wren: My son composed the inscription. I think my reputation is safe now. And so is the cathedral itself: if you want to know what that strange, thin man was doing yesterday evening, after he crept in here quietly, I can reassure you. He had no explosives. He looked like an anguished soul, not like a good Christian, but he came here to pray. I watched him. And I'm sure you'll find out what was troubling his conscience. I'll show you out, and wish you good luck.

Standing once again by the statue of Queen Anne in front of the steps that lead up to the cathedral, Holmes and Watson confer about their next move.

Watson: Everywhere we've been, at all these historic buildings, we've found that ghosts from the past are on guard. They scared away that mysterious villain, and they're still keeping watch. Perhaps the prime minister's fears are misplaced.

Holmes: In Ye Olde Cheshire Cheese we got an important clue. Jim Barnes, who met the suspicious bearded man there, is working in the engine house of the new bridge, although we were told that Jim is work-shy – and stoking boilers is certainly no job for the idle. Now tell me, Watson, where can there be no guardian spirit from days of old?

Watson: In a new building!

Holmes: My dear Watson, you've grasped it! Our next stop is Tower Bridge. We must hurry, as it's getting dark already. We'll take a cab.

hier ist berühmt: «Wenn du ein Denkmal suchst, schaue dich um.»

Wren: Mein Sohn hat diese Inschrift verfasst. Mein Ruf ist mittlerweile gesichert. Die Kirche auch: Wenn Sie wissen möchten, was der merkwürdige, dünne Mann wollte, der sich gestern Abend hier einschlich, dann kann ich Sie beruhigen. Er brachte keinen Sprengstoff mit. Er sah wie eine gequälte Seele aus, nicht wie ein guter Christ, aber er kam zum Beten. Sie werden sicher herausfinden, was er auf dem Gewissen hat. Ich wünsche Ihnen viel Erfolg und begleite Sie zum Ausgang.

Holmes und Watson stehen wieder vor der Statue der Königin Anne an den Stufen vor dem Eingang zur Kathedrale und beraten sich über die nächsten Schritte.

Watson: Überall, wo wir hinkamen, an all den historischen Orten, passen die Geister der Vergangenheit auf. Sie haben diesen mysteriösen Bösewicht in die Flucht geschlagen und stehen immer noch Wache. Vielleicht sind die Befürchtungen des Premierministers unberechtigt.

Holmes: Wir haben im Ye Olde Cheshire Cheese einen wichtigen Hinweis erhalten. Jim Barnes, der den Verdächtigen dort wohl getroffen hat, arbeitet im Maschinenraum der neuen Brücke. Uns wurde gesagt, dass Jim Arbeit scheue, aber dort zu heizen ist mit Sicherheit kein Job für Faule. Jetzt sagen Sie mir, Watson, wo kann es keinen alten Schutzgeist geben?

Watson: In einem modernen Bauwerk!

Holmes: Ganz richtig, lieber Watson! Wir fahren zur Tower Bridge. Wir müssen uns beeilen, es wird schon dunkel. Wir nehmen eine Droschke.

13.

A Marvel of Technology
(Tower Bridge)

Ein technisches Wunder
(Tower Bridge)

Dark and impenetrable at night, like the face of a forest, is the London waterside.

From *The Mirror of the Sea*, Joseph Conrad

The striking silhouette and unusual mechanism of Tower Bridge make it one of London's best-known landmarks. Twenty years of planning and construction preceded the opening ceremony on 30 June 1894. In a period when the city was growing rapidly and the East End was severely overcrowded, a new river crossing on this stretch of the Thames was long overdue. There were already several bridges further west, but none to the east of London Bridge. The task of easing congestion by building a new bridge was difficult, as it was essential not to impede shipping: the Thames quayside between the Tower of London and London Bridge was still used for loading and unloading large vessels. The city needed a bridge that could carry thousands of vehicles and 25,000 pedestrians per day across the river, but at the same time allow ships with a height of 43 metres between the water surface and the tip of their masts to pass, even at high tide. A competition was held, and the winning entry was submitted by Sir Horace Jones, architect and surveyor to the City of London. He proposed a novel combination of a drawbridge and a suspension bridge. Piers grounded in the river bed support two towers, each 65 metres tall. Between these and two smaller towers, one each on the north and the south bank, massive chains are suspended to bear the weight of the north and

Dunkel und undurchdringlich bei Nacht, wie das Antlitz
eines Waldes, ist das Londoner Flussufer.

Aus ‹Der Spiegel der See›, Joseph Conrad

Die markante Form und der ungewöhnliche Mechanismus
der Tower Bridge machen sie zu einem der bekanntesten
Wahrzeichen Londons. Der feierlichen Eröffnung am
30. Juni 1894 ging eine zwanzigjährige Planungs- und
Bauphase voraus. Eine neue Überquerung an dieser
Stelle der Themse war längst überfällig geworden. Die
Stadt wuchs damals in rasantem Tempo, die Wohnviertel
im East End platzten aus allen Nähten. Es gab bereits
etliche Brücken weiter westlich, aber keine feste Verbindung östlich von London Bridge. Aber der Schiffsverkehr durfte durch einen Brückenbau nicht beeinträchtigt
werden, da die Themseufer zwischen dem Tower of
London und London Bridge für das Beladen und Ent-
laden großer Handelsschiffe genutzt wurden.
Die Stadt bedurfte einer Konstruktion, die einer-
seits viele Tausend Fahrzeuge und 25 000 Fußgänger
täglich auf der Brücke, und andererseits Schiffe mit
43 Meter Höhe zwischen Wasserfläche und Mastspitze
auch bei Flut passieren ließ. Bei einem Wettbewerb
gewann der Vorschlag des Stadtbaumeisters Sir Horace
Jones. Er sah eine neuartige Kombination aus Klapp-
und Hängebrücke vor. Mitten im Flussbett verankerte
Pfeiler stützen zwei 65 Meter hohe Türme. Zwischen
diesen und zwei kleineren Türmen am Nord- bzw. Südufer sind massive Ketten gespannt, die den nördlichen
und den südlichen Abschnitt nach dem Prinzip einer

south sections of the bridge. The middle section consists of two moving arms, known as bascules, which can be raised until they are almost vertical. The structure directly above the bascules, spanning the gap between the tops of the two tall towers, was conceived as a footbridge at a dizzying height, but also serves an important structural purpose: it braces the towers against the lateral pull of the suspension-bridge sections on the north and south sides.

To make the bridge fit in with its surroundings, especially the Tower of London, it was clad in expensive Cornish granite and Portland limestone, and Gothic-style decoration was added, which some contemporary critics thought ridiculous. However, the pseudo-medieval trappings of Tower Bridge contributed to its unmistakeable form and thus to its fame.

From the very beginning, Tower Bridge was a magnet for visitors, and also for adventurers. In 1912 a pilot flew his biplane between the towers, and in 1968 even a fighter jet of the Royal Air Force achieved this manoeuvre. In 2003 the American magician David Blaine had himself locked into a glass cage that was hoisted aloft in full public view next to the bridge, and stayed there without food for 44 days. However, the most astounding stunt was unintentional: in 1952 the safety measures normally taken to close Tower Bridge to traffic failed, and the bascules began to rise while a number 78 bus full of passengers was still on the bridge. The driver put his foot down and cleared the gap.

Hängebrücke tragen. Der mittlere Abschnitt besteht aus zwei beweglichen Teilen, «Baskülen» genannt, die beinahe senkrecht hochgeklappt werden können. Die Verbindung zwischen den hohen Türmen, direkt über den Baskülen, dient nicht nur als Fußgängerweg in schwindelerregender Höhe, sondern hat auch eine wichtige statische Funktion: Dadurch stützen sich die Türme gegenseitig gegen die seitlichen Züge der nördlichen und südlichen Abschnitte der Hängebrücke. Damit die Erscheinung der Brücke zur Umgebung, vor allem zum benachbarten Tower of London passte, erhielt sie eine steinerne Verkleidung aus teuren Materialien – Granit aus Cornwall und Kalkstein aus Portland – und Verzierungen im gotischen Stil, was einige zeitgenössische Kritiker als absurd bezeichneten. Die mittelalterliche Anmutung der Tower Bridge trug aber zu ihrer unverwechselbaren Silhouette und so zu ihrem Ruhm bei. Von Anfang an zog die Tower Bridge Besucher, aber auch Abenteurer in ihren Bann. 1912 flog ein Pilot seinen Doppeldecker zwischen den Türmen hindurch, 1968 schaffte sogar ein Jagdflugzeug der Royal Air Force das Wagnis. 2003 ließ sich der amerikanische Zauberkünstler David Blaine 44 Tage lang ohne Nahrung und für alle sichtbar in einem neben der Brücke aufgehängten Glaskasten einsperren. Das erstaunlichste Kunststück geschah jedoch unfreiwillig im Jahr 1952: Weil die Sicherheitsmaßnahmen, die Tower Bridge für den Verkehr abzuriegeln, versagten, begann das Hochklappen der Baskülen, während ein vollbesetzter Bus der Linie 78 über die Brücke fuhr. Der Fahrer gab Gas und schaffte den Sprung.

The road is still regularly raised for ships (for times see www.towerbridge.org.uk), since 1976 with power provided by oil and electricity rather than steam. In 1910 the high-level walkway between the towers was closed, as pedestrians preferred to wait below until the bascules had been lowered again. In 1982 this walkway was opened to visitors, who can see an exhibition about the bridge and enjoy panoramic views before descending to visit the impressive boilers and the original steam engines.

The hansom cab carrying Holmes and Watson from St Paul's Cathedral rounds the Tower of London and approaches Tower Bridge.

Holmes: We have to cross the bridge. The engine room is on the south bank. Look! Can you see the two men ahead of us on the pavement? One is tall and thin as a rake, the other one has a stocky build. It's getting too dark now for me to tell whether he has red hair, but I think we've found our suspects.
Watson: The bell is ringing – we've arrived too late! They're raising the bridge.

At that moment the roadway is closed, right in front of their cab. 50 metres further ahead, the two men whom Holmes has spotted are among the last pedestrians who cross. Watson jumps out and runs to the guards, who have drawn a metal gate across the road to block access to the middle part of the bridge. He talks to one of them and waves his arms excitedly, but the gate remains closed.

Seit 1976 mit Öl und Elektrik statt mit Dampf betrieben, wird die Fahrbahn regelmäßig für Schiffe hochgeklappt (Zeiten siehe www.towerbridge.org.uk). 1910 wurden die erhöhten Stege zwischen den Brückentürmen geschlossen, da Fußgänger lieber unten warteten, bis die Baskülen wieder heruntergeklappt waren. Seit 1982 können Besucher dort eine Ausstellung besichtigen und den Panoramablick genießen, bevor sie nach dem Abstieg die eindrucksvollen alten Dampfkessel und Dampfmaschinen bestaunen.

Die Droschke fährt Holmes und Watson von St Paul's aus am Tower of London vorbei und nähert sich der Tower Bridge.

Holmes: Wir müssen die Brücke überqueren. Der Maschinenraum ist am Südufer. Sehen Sie diese beiden Männer vor uns auf dem Gehweg? Einer ist spindeldürr und hochgewachsen, der andere stämmig – bei der Dämmerung kann ich aus dieser Entfernung nicht mehr erkennen, ob er rote Haare hat. Aber ich denke, wir haben unsere Verdächtigen gefunden.

Watson: Und es bimmelt – wir kommen zu spät! Sie ziehen die Brücke hoch.

In diesem Augenblick wird direkt vor ihrer Droschke die Fahrbahn gesperrt. Die beiden verdächtigen Männer haben 50 Meter Vorsprung und sind unter den letzten Fußgängern, die passieren dürfen. Watson springt aus der Kutsche und rennt auf die Wachposten zu, die das Metalltor auf der Zufahrt zum Mittelteil der Brücke schließen. Er redet zu einem von ihnen und gestikuliert aufgeregt, aber das Tor bleibt geschlossen.

Watson (returning red-faced): The gatekeeper is an insolent wretch. I told him that the great detective Sherlock Holmes is sitting in this hansom cab and has to pass through immediately on urgent government business. He laughed at me. He said "And I'm Professor Moriarty – no-one is crossing this bridge." But we can go up to the high-level footbridge. The lift to the top only takes a minute.

Holmes: Please be calm, Watson. We'll save no time by crossing on the elevated passageway – the road down here will be open again in five minutes. Besides, we know where those two are heading. While we wait, I'll review what I know about the bridge. I once made the acquaintance of the architect, Sir Horace Jones. He was one of my first clients, and I was able to help him in an embarrassing matter. Unfortunately he died ten years ago. I'm familiar with some details of the lifting mechanism. Steam engines generate hydraulic power, which is stored in vast accumulators. They provide the force to drive motors that lie hidden in the bridge piers. These motors then turn a huge mechanism to which the bascules are attached. The roadway rotates into a vertical position, while the counterweights move downwards into chambers below the towers. The whole bridge is an extremely robust steel structure – even the towers, which look as if they are made of stone. To destroy it, an enormous explosion would be needed.

Watson: Holmes, your mastery of the facts never ceases to amaze me!

Holmes: No great learning was necessary in this case, Watson: all of that was printed in *The Times* a year ago, when the bridge was inaugurated. The article heaped praise

Watson *(kehrt mit einem roten Gesicht zurück)*: Der Tormann ist ein frecher Hund. Ich sagte ihm, in dieser Droschke sitzt der große Detektiv Sherlock Holmes und muss in einer dringenden Staatsangelegenheit sofort vorbei. Er lachte nur und sagte: «Und ich bin Professor Moriarty – niemand überquert diese Brücke.» Aber wir können die Fußgängerverbindung oben nehmen. Der Aufzug braucht nur eine Minute.

Holmes: Alles mit der Ruhe, Watson. Mit dem Höhenweg sparen wir keine Zeit. Innerhalb fünf Minuten ist die Straße hier unten wieder geöffnet. Außerdem wissen wir, wo die beiden hingehen. Während wir warten, sortiere ich mein Wissen über diese Brücke. Ich kannte den Architekten, Sir Horace Jones – er gehörte zu meinen ersten Klienten. Ich konnte ihm in einer heiklen Angelegenheit helfen. Leider verstarb er vor gut zehn Jahren. Ich erinnere mich an einige Einzelheiten des Hebemechanismus. Dampfmaschinen erzeugen hydraulischen Druck, der in großen Akkumulatoren gespeichert wird. Diese liefern die Kraft für den Antrieb von Motoren unter den Türmen. Die Motoren bewegen einen mächtigen Drehmechanismus: Die Baskülen klappen mit der Fahrbahn hoch, die Gegengewichte drehen nach unten in Kammern unter den Türmen. Die gesamte Brücke ist eine stabile Stahlkonstruktion – auch die Türme, obwohl sie aussehen, als wären sie aus Stein. Um sie zu zerstören, wäre eine gewaltige Explosion nötig.

Watson: Es erstaunt mich immer wieder, was Sie alles wissen, Holmes!

Holmes: In diesem Fall hat es nichts mit Wissen zu tun, Watson. Das war alles vor einem Jahr in ‹The Times› zu lesen, als die Einweihung stattfand. Der Artikel pries die tech-

on the technical ingenuity of the engineers. But in fact the moving parts, rather than the bridge structure itself, would be the weak point. Imagine what would happen if someone disabled the mechanism just at the moment when the bascules were neither fully raised nor fully lowered. River traffic to the Port of London and road traffic across the bridge would both come to a standstill. Half the city would be paralysed. Well, the gatekeepers are opening up, and we can move on at last. We'll get out as soon as we reach the south bank. I recall that there are steps down to the engine room. Keep your revolver at the ready.

The cab halts at Holmes' command on the far side of the bridge, and the two rush down stone steps to the riverbank. There, at the entrance to the engine house, they see a stout middle-aged man with a broad, bearded face. He holds a key in his hand.

Holmes: Watson, I was mistaken. I thought ghosts were only found in old buildings. That's Sir Horace.

Sir Horace Jones: Mr Holmes, I'm pleased to see you again! You needn't be surprised to see me here. I keep an eye on my bridge. This is the first anniversary of the opening, and it goes without saying that, today of all days, I'm making sure everything is as it should be. And would you believe it? I've just caught two wrong-doers who were preparing an outrage against the bridge. I've been watching them for several days. One of them works here as a stoker. I observed that he had brought boxes into the coal store and hidden them there. I examined the boxes yesterday, and what did I find? Dynamite! And then last night the stoker sneaked in with another man – a nasty-looking

nische Konstruktion als geniale Leistung. Es sind aber die beweglichen Teile, nicht die Bauweise der Brücke, die eine Schwachstelle darstellen. Stellen Sie sich vor, jemand setzt den Mechanismus in dem Augenblick außer Betrieb, wenn die Baskülen weder ganz oben noch ganz unten sind. Dann käme der Schiffsverkehr auf dem Weg zum Londoner Hafen und der Verkehr auf der Brücke zum Stillstand. Die halbe Stadt wäre lahmgelegt. Jetzt öffnet der Wachposten, und wir können endlich weiter. Wir steigen aus, sobald wir am Südufer sind. Dort gibt es, glaube ich, eine Treppe zum Maschinenraum hinunter. Halten Sie Ihren Revolver bereit.

Auf Holmes' Anweisung hin hält die Droschke auf der anderen Seite der Brücke. Die zwei eilen über die Steintreppe zum Ufer hinunter. Am Eingang zum Krafthaus sehen sie einen kräftigen Mann mittleren Alters mit einem breiten, bärtigem Gesicht und einem Schlüssel in der Hand.

Holmes: Watson, so kann man sich irren. Ich dachte, Geister wären nur in alten Häusern zu finden. Das ist Sir Horace.

Sir Horace Jones: Mr Holmes, es freut mich, Sie wiederzusehen! Wundern Sie sich nicht, dass ich hier stehe. Ich habe ein Auge auf meine Brücke. Heute jährt sich die Eröffnung zum ersten Mal – klar, dass ich gerade heute nach dem Rechten schaue. Ich habe soeben zwei Verbrecher, die einen Anschlag auf die Brücke planten, auf frischer Tat ertappt. Ich beobachte sie seit einigen Tagen. Einer arbeitet hier als Heizer. Ich habe gesehen, wie er Kisten im Vorratsraum unter den Kohlehalden versteckt. Gestern untersuchte ich die Kisten, und was fand ich? Dynamit! Gestern Abend kam der Heizer heimlich mit einem anderen – ein unangenehmer Typ, hochgewachsen, spindeldürr, mit einem schwarzen

character, tall and thin with a black beard and a penetrating stare – and together they took a long, close look at the steam engines. I do believe they intended to blow up the engine room! They won't succeed now, though.

Holmes: Why? What have you done with them?

Sir Horace Jones *(holds up the key)*: It was very simple! A couple of minutes ago they went into the store to retrieve their boxes from beneath the coal. I locked them in. Now they're behind a thick oak door, and they'll not succeed in breaking it down.

Watson: Bravo! You've saved London from disaster.

Sir Horace Jones: Do you think I would stand by and watch while the pinnacle of my life's work was destroyed? The Prince of Wales opened the bridge exactly a year ago. Thousands came and cheered. They could see that my bridge is a new wonder of the world. It was a colossal enterprise, and took eight years to build. We used 11,000 tons of steel and unimaginable quantities of stone. The bridge is strong and stable, but its operation depends on the lifting mechanism. How could I fail to guard the engine room?

The architect smiles. Suddenly several shots ring out in quick succession.

Sir Horace Jones *(turns to the door behind him, and pushes it open)*: Could they be escaping? Holmes, you must stop them. The coal store, where I locked them in, is down that corridor on the left.

Through the open door Holmes and Watson peer into a long, ill-lit passage. Watson takes out his revolver.

Bart und stechendem Blick – und sie schauten sich gemeinsam die Dampfmaschinen näher an. Ich bin sicher, dass sie den Maschinenraum in die Luft sprengen wollten. Jetzt wird es ihnen aber nicht mehr gelingen.

Holmes: Warum? Was haben Sie mit ihnen gemacht?

Sir Horace Jones *(hält seinen Schlüssel hoch)*: Ganz einfach! Sie gingen vor drei Minuten in das Kohlenlager, um ihre Kisten zu holen. Ich habe sie dort eingesperrt. Nun sind sie hinter einer starken Eichentür, die sie nicht aufbrechen können.

Watson: Bravo! Sie haben London vor einer Katastrophe bewahrt.

Sir Horace Jones: Meinen Sie, ich würde einfach dastehen und mit ansehen, wie ein Teil meines Lebenswerks zerstört wird? Heute vor genau einem Jahr hat der Prinz von Wales meine Brücke eröffnet. Tausende kamen und jubelten, weil sie verstanden, dass die Brücke ein neues Weltwunder ist. Der Aufwand war groß: acht Jahre Bauzeit, 11 000 Tonnen Stahl, Unmengen an Stein. Die Brücke ist stabil, doch ihr Betrieb hängt ganz von der Hebetechnik ab. Selbstverständlich lasse ich keinen Anschlag auf den Maschinenraum zu.

Der Architekt lächelt zufrieden. Plötzlich ertönen einige Schüsse schnell hintereinander.

Sir Horace Jones *(dreht sich zur Tür und schiebt sie auf)*: Nicht, dass sie entkommen! Holmes, Sie müssen es verhindern. Das Kohlenlager, in dem ich sie eingesperrt habe, ist den linken Korridor hinunter.

Holmes und Watson schauen durch die Tür in einen langen, schummrigen Gang. Watson zieht seinen Revolver.

Holmes: I can hear footsteps – from a single person. One is them is getting away. Careful, Watson. We'll move forwards slowly until we come to the coal store. This could be a trap. The second man may be armed and lying in wait for us.

They creep along the dark corridor.

Holmes: There's somebody on the floor! Ahead of us on the left. I can see an outstretched arm.

They hurry a few paces further and see a man lying on his stomach in a doorway. He groans. Behind him coal is piled high. Watson bends over the man.

Watson: He's been wounded in the head. His hair is covered in blood. It looks serious.
Holmes: Despite all the blood, I can see that his hair is naturally red. This is the stoker Jim Barnes. Now look at the lock. The other man fired on it to open the door. Then he shot his accomplice in the head from behind and made his escape alone. He wants to avoid recognition, so he made sure that Barnes can't betray him. We'll follow him, Watson. He has to be stopped!

They run along the corridor to the engine room, where a huge steam engine hisses softly as wheels and pistons slowly move. No-one is to be seen there. Holmes feels a cool breath of air on his cheek and realises that a window high in the wall is open. With two strides he reaches the spot, and Watson helps him up.

Holmes: Ich höre Schritte, aber nur von einer Person. Einer von ihnen entkommt uns. Vorsicht, Watson. Wir tasten uns langsam voran, bis wir zum Kohlenlager kommen. Es könnte eine Falle sein. Der zweite Mann ist vielleicht bewaffnet und lauert uns auf.

Sie schleichen durch den dunklen Gang.

Holmes: Da liegt jemand! Auf dem Boden vorne links – ich sehe einen ausgestreckten Arm.

Sie eilen einige Meter nach vorne und sehen, dass in einer offenen Tür ein Mann auf dem Bauch liegt. Er stöhnt. Hinter ihm türmt sich eine Kohlenhalde auf. Watson beugt sich über den Mann.

Watson: Er hat eine Kopfwunde. Seine Haare sind voller Blut – es sieht nach einer schweren Verletzung aus.

Holmes: Trotzdem sehe ich, dass er rotes Haar hat. Das ist der Heizer Jim Barnes. Und schauen Sie sich das Schloss an. Mit gezielten Schüssen hat der zweite Mann die Tür aufgebrochen. Danach hat er seinem Komplizen von hinten in den Kopf geschossen und ist alleine geflohen. Er möchte unerkannt bleiben und sorgte dafür, dass Barnes ihn nicht verraten kann. Hinterher, Watson, wir müssen ihn zur Strecke bringen!

Sie laufen durch den dunklen Gang zum Maschinenraum. Eine riesige Dampfmaschine zischt leise. Räder und Kolben bewegen sich langsam, aber kein Mensch hält sich im Raum auf. Holmes spürt einen kühlen Windhauch im Gesicht und bemerkt, dass ein Fenster oben in der Wand geöffnet ist. Mit zwei schnellen Schritten erreicht er die Stelle. Watson stützt

Holmes pulls himself onto the window ledge, climbs nimbly through the opening and jumps to the ground on the outside. He is on the side of the engine house that faces away from the river. As he looks about him, the shrill blast of a boat's whistle sounds. Holmes sprints around the building to the river bank and sees a steam tug that is already twenty metres from the quayside and is heading downriver fast. Black smoke is pouring from its funnel, and at the stern of the tug a tall, haggard figure is shaking a fist at him.

Holmes stands still for a moment, directing a keen gaze at the steam tug. At his feet waves slap against the quay. Reflections from lights on the bridge and passing ships dance in the turbulent black water. Holmes turns away and walks to the engine house, where he finds Watson and Sir Horace Jones at the door.

Holmes: Sir Horace, your vigorous action foiled the plans of a desperate man. Watson, will you use your professional skills? Perhaps there is a chance of saving Barnes. I'll tell the bridge keeper to alert the river police and Scotland Yard. The unknown villain won't evade capture a second time. The name of the boat on which he is fleeing was visible: the White Raven. He may be dangerous and energetic, and he may have planned his escape carefully, but he is no criminal genius. He leaves tell-tale clues everywhere. I can inform the prime minister that the immediate threat has been averted. And later we'll see whether Dr Conan Doyle thinks this case is worthy of publication.

ihn, und Holmes zieht sich mit einem kräftigen Ruck auf das Fensterbrett, klettert flink durch die Öffnung und springt nach draußen. Er befindet sich auf der hinteren, dem Fluss abgewandten Seite des Krafthauses. Als er sich umsieht, hört Holmes das laute, schrille Pfeifen eines Boots. Er rennt um das Haus zum Flussufer und sieht einen Dampfschlepper, der sich bereits zwanzig Meter vom Kai entfernt hat und mit rauchendem Schlot schnell in östliche Richtung zieht. Eine große, magere Gestalt am Heck reckt ihm eine Faust entgegen.

Holmes bleibt einen Augenblick stehen und richtet seinen scharfen Blick auf den Schlepper. Zu seinen Füßen schwappen Wellen gegen die Kaimauer. Die Lichter der Brücke und der vorbeifahrenden Schiffe spiegeln sich tänzelnd im unruhigen schwarzen Wasser. Holmes kehrt zum Krafthaus zurück, wo er Watson und Sir Horace Jones vor der Tür antrifft.

Holmes: Ihr beherztes Eingreifen hat den Plan eines verzweifelten Mannes vereitelt, Sir Horace. Watson, nutzen Sie Ihre Expertise und schauen Sie, ob Barnes zu retten ist. Ich werde die Brückenwächter anweisen, die Wasserschutzpolizei und Scotland Yard zu holen. Der unbekannte Bösewicht wird uns nicht noch einmal durch das Netz schlüpfen. Ich konnte den Namen des Bootes erkennen, auf dem er geflohen ist: «White Raven». Der Mann ist zwar gefährlich und tatkräftig und hat seinen Fluchtweg gut geplant, aber ein kriminelles Genie ist er nicht. Überall hat er verräterische Spuren hinterlassen. Ich kann den Premierminister informieren, dass die unmittelbare Gefahr gebannt ist. Und wir werden sehen, ob dieser Fall Herrn Conan Doyle eine Veröffentlichung wert ist.

The Detectives
and their Witnesses

Die Ermittler und ihre Zeugen

Sherlock Holmes and Dr Watson Dr Watson's accounts
of Holmes' cases reveal sporadic details of the life of
the great detective, but leave significant gaps in the
story. Holmes was probably born in 1854. After carrying out his first criminal investigations while still at
university, he took up the profession of "consulting
detective" and met the young doctor John H. Watson
when looking for someone to share his rooms in Baker
Street. After several successful years of detective work,
Holmes disappeared following his supposed death
in 1891 in combat with his mortal enemy Professor
Moriarty at the Reichenbach Falls in Switzerland. By
his own account he travelled in Europe and to Tibet,
Persia and Arabia in these years. In spring 1894, just
over twelve months before the events described in this
book, he returned to London and pursued his former
activities for several more years. In the early 20th century he retired and devoted himself to beekeeping in
rural Sussex. The date of his death is not known.

Prince Albert of Saxe-Coburg and Gotha (1819–
1861), who bore the title Prince Consort after
his marriage to Queen Victoria in 1840, worked
for educational reform and the abolition of
child labour and slavery. He took a leading
role in organising the Great Exhibition of 1851.
Albert and Victoria spoke and wrote to each
other in German and English. He died at Windsor Castle and was buried in the mausoleum at
Frogmore nearby.

Sherlock Holmes und Dr. Watson Dr. Watsons Aufzeichnungen von Holmes' Fällen verraten einiges über das Leben des Detektivs, lassen aber erhebliche Lücken. Holmes kam wahrscheinlich 1854 zur Welt. Nach ersten kriminalistischen Ermittlungen während des Studiums arbeitete er als «beratender Detektiv» und lernte den jungen Arzt Dr. John H. Watson kennen, weil er einen Mitbewohner für seine Wohnung in der Baker Street suchte. Es folgten Jahre erfolgreicher Detektivarbeit. Nach seinem angeblichen Tod 1891 im Kampf mit seinem Erzfeind Professor Moriarty an den Reichenbachfällen in der Schweiz verschwand Holmes drei Jahre lang. Nach eigenen Angaben bereiste er in dieser Zeit Europa, Tibet, Persien und Arabien. Im Frühling 1894, etwas mehr als zwölf Monate vor den hier beschriebenen Ereignissen, tauchte er wieder in London auf. Nach weiteren Jahren als Detektiv setzte er sich Anfang des 20. Jhs. in der Grafschaft Sussex zur Ruhe und widmete sich der Bienenzucht im ländlichen Sussex. Sein Todesdatum ist unbekannt.

Prinz Albert Albert von Sachsen-Coburg und Gotha (1819–1861) führte den Titel Prinzgemahl seit seiner Ehe mit Königin Victoria im Jahr 1840 und setzte sich für Bildungsreformen und die Abschaffung von Kinderarbeit und der Sklaverei ein. Er war an der Organisation der Great Exhibition von 1851, der ersten Weltausstellung, federführend beteiligt. Albert und Victoria sprachen und schrieben auf Deutsch und Englisch untereinander. Er starb auf Schloss Windsor und wurde im Mausoleum im nahe gelegenen Frogmore beigesetzt.

George Frederic Handel (1685–1759), born in Halle, Germany under the name of Georg Friedrich Händel, came to London in 1712 and took British citizenship. In addition to his *Coronation Anthems* and famous works such as the *Water Music*, *Music for the Royal Fireworks* and *The Messiah*, he enjoyed great success as a composer of operas and oratorios. From 1723 until his death he lived in Mayfair at number 25 Brook Street, which can be visited: Handel and Hendrix (Mon – Sat 11 am – 6 pm).

Mary, Queen of Scots (1542–1587) was executed at Fotheringay Castle after 18 years of captivity in English castles and aristocratic houses. She was buried in Peterborough Cathedral. Her son James VI of Scotland had her mortal remains transferred to Westminster Abbey after becoming James I of England.

Elizabeth Nightingale (1704–1731), the daughter of Earl Ferrers, married a clergyman and bore two sons. She died giving birth to a daughter, also called Elizabeth.

Guy Fawkes (1570–1606), who came from York, fought in the Netherlands in the armies of the Spanish king. Later he joined the Roman Catholic conspirators who planned to blow up Parliament at its opening ceremony in 1605 and restore the Catholic religion in England. Guy Fawkes Day on 5 November commemorates the discovery of

Georg Friedrich Händel (1685–1759), geboren in Halle, siedelte 1712 nach London über und nahm die britische Staatsbürgerschaft an. Abgesehen von seinen Krönungshymnen und bekannten Werken wie die ‹Wassermusik›, ‹Feuerwerksmusik› und den ‹Messias›, genoss er großen Ruhm als Komponist von Opern und Oratorien. Von 1723 bis zu seinem Tod wohnte er im Stadtteil Mayfair in der Brook Street Nr. 25, das Besuchern zugänglich ist: Handel and Hendrix (Mo. – Sa. 10–18 Uhr).

Maria Stuart (englisch: Mary, Queen of Scots, 1542–1587) wurde nach 18 Jahren Gefangenschaft in englischen Herrensitzen auf Burg Fotheringay enthauptet und in der Kathedrale von Peterborough beigesetzt. Ihr Sohn, König James I. von England, gleichzeitig auch bekannt als James VI. von Schottland, ließ ihre Gebeine in die Westminster Abbey überführen.

Elizabeth Nightingale (1704–1731), Tochter des Grafen Ferrers, heiratete einen Geistlichen, gebar zwei Söhne und starb bei der Geburt ihrer Tochter, die ebenfalls Elizabeth hieß.

Guy Fawkes (1570–1606) aus York kämpfte in den Niederlanden auf der Seite des katholischen Spaniens. Später schloss er sich den katholischen Verschwörern an, die 1605 das Parlament am Tag der Sessionseröffnung in die Luft sprengen und die katholische Kirche in England wieder an die Macht bringen wollten. Die Aufdeckung des Komplotts wird jährlich am 5. November, dem «Guy Fawkes

the plot with the burning of a straw effigy (Guy) and fireworks. Discrimination of Catholics has still not been fully abolished in the United Kingdom, as the monarch, being head of the Church of England, may not be Catholic or marry a Catholic.

Ben Caunt (1815–1861), a bare-knuckle prize fighter from Nottinghamshire, became heavyweight champion of England in 1841 and fought his last boxing match in 1857. He was also the landlord of the Coach and Horses pub in St Martin's Lane in London.

Sir George Downing (1623–1684) was born in Dublin. When he was a child, the family emigrated to America, and in 1642 he was one of the earliest graduates of Harvard College, which later became Harvard University. After returning to England he served both Oliver Cromwell and Charles II as a diplomat and financial expert. He took a major role in the purchase by the English Crown of New Amsterdam (now New York) from the Netherlands, and engaged in deals that made him a wealthy landowner.

Lord Salisbury Robert Gascoyne-Cecil, 3rd Marquis of Salisbury, was a scion of a noble family whose tradition of serving in high offices of state began in the 16th century and continued until recent years (Viscount Cranbourne, 7th Marquis of Salisbury, was Leader of the House of Lords until 1998). With one interruption (1892–1895), Lord Salisbury was prime minister from 1885 until 1902. He was the last holder of the office who

Day», mit einem Feuerwerk und dem Verbrennen einer Strohpuppe («Guy») gefeiert. Die Diskriminierung von Katholiken in Großbritannien wurde bis heute nicht restlos beseitigt: Der Monarch darf als Oberhaupt der Church of England weder katholisch sein noch eine(n) katholische(n) Partner(in) heiraten.

Ben Caunt (1815–1861), ein Bare-Knuckle-Boxer aus Nottinghamshire, wurde 1841 englischer Meister im Schwergewicht und boxte zum letzten Mal im Jahr 1857. Er war auch Wirt der Kneipe Coach and Horses in der St Martin's Lane in London.

Sir George Downing (1623–1684) wurde in Dublin geboren, kam als Kind mit seinen Eltern nach Amerika und gehörte 1642 zum ersten Absolventenjahrgang des Harvard College, der späteren Harvard University. Nach seiner Rückkehr nach England stand er als Diplomat und Finanzfachmann im Dienst von Oliver Cromwell und Charles II., war am Kauf von Neu Amsterdam (heute: New York) von den Niederlanden maßgeblich beteiligt und wurde dank seiner Geschäfte zum wohlhabenden Grundbesitzer.

Lord Salisbury Robert Gascoyne-Cecil, 3. Marquis von Salisbury, entstammte einer Adelsfamilie, die in Tradition seit dem 16. Jh. bis heute im Staatsdienst tätig ist (Viscount Cranbourne, 7. Marquis von Salisbury, war bis 1998 Vorsitzender des House of Lords). Mit einer Unterbrechung (1892–1895) war Lord Salisbury von 1885 bis 1902 Premierminister – der letzte, der nicht in Downing Street Nr. 10 wohnte, da er seine Residenz in

did not live in Downing Street, preferring the family residence in Arlington Street in St James's or his country seat, Hatfield House, where his descendants still live.

King Charles I displayed better judgment and a worthier demeanour at his execution than in governing his kingdom. On the scaffold he declared "I go from a corruptible to an incorruptible crown, where no disturbance can be." As a defender of the episcopal church against Puritans who were opposed to the office of bishop, in 1660 he was the last saint to be canonised by the Church of England, which still officially regards him as a martyr.

Daniel Briggs represents all the nameless workers who built London and its great monuments.

Lord Nelson Horatio Nelson (1758–1805) joined the Royal Navy at the age of twelve. In 1781 he was appointed captain of a frigate. From 1793 he fought in the Mediterranean, the Atlantic and the Baltic against France and its allies in the Revolutionary and Napoleonic Wars. He lost the sight in his right eye when attacking Calvi on the island of Corsica. In 1797 he was wounded in fighting at Santa Cruz on Tenerife, and lost his right arm. By destroying the French fleet at the Battle of the Nile in 1798, he thwarted Napoleon's plans to conquer Egypt and the Near East. Nelson's victories and reckless disregard for his own safety made him a hero and legend in his own lifetime. He is also popularly known for his affair with Lady Hamilton, the wife of the British ambassador in Naples.

der Arlington Street in St James's und den Landsitz Hatfield House, wo seine Nachkommen noch heute leben, bevorzugte.

König Charles I. zeigte bei seiner Hinrichtung mehr Augenmaß und Würde als bei seinen Regierungsgeschäften. Auf dem Schafott erklärte er: «Ich gehe von einer vergänglichen zu einer unvergänglichen Krone.» Als ein Verteidiger der Bischofskirche gegenüber den Puritanern, die das Bischofsamt entschieden ablehnten, wurde er 1660 als Letzter von der anglikanischen Kirche heiliggesprochen und wird noch immer als Märtyrer betrachtet.

Daniel Briggs steht hier stellvertretend für alle namenlosen Arbeiter, die London und seine Denkmäler bauten.

Lord Nelson Horatio Nelson (1758–1805) trat mit zwölf Jahren in die königliche Marine ein und wurde 1781 Kapitän einer Fregatte. Ab 1793 kämpfte er im Mittelmeer, im Atlantik und in der Ostsee gegen Frankreich und dessen Alliierte in den Revolutions- und Napoleonischen Kriegen. Bei der Erstürmung von Calvi auf Korsika verlor er das Sehvermögen auf dem rechten Auge, 1797 seinen rechten Arm bei einem Angriff auf Santa Cruz de Tenerife. Seine Vernichtung der französischen Flotte 1798 in der Bucht von Abukir vereitelte Napoleons Versuch, Ägypten und den Nahen Osten zu erobern. Nelsons Siege und rücksichtslose Missachtung der eigenen Sicherheit machten ihn zu Lebzeiten zum Volkshelden. Er ist auch gemeinhin bekannt für seine Affäre mit Lady Hamilton, der Frau des britischen Botschafters in Neapel. Nach seinem Tod bei der Schlacht von Trafalgar

After his death at the Battle of Trafalgar, his body was taken back to London in a cask filled with brandy and laid in a marble sarcophagus in St Paul's Cathedral in the presence of 32 admirals and more than 100 ships' captains. He suffered from sea sickness all his life.

Eliza Doolittle Covent Garden is still a theatre district. The idea for the play *Pygmalion*, which was later re-worked as the musical *My Fair Lady*, came to George Bernard Shaw in 1897, two years after the events in this book. When Sherlock Holmes came to question her, Eliza Doolittle therefore had no idea that one day the professor of phonetics Henry Higgins would teach her to lose her Cockney accent and that she would learn to pronounce English like a fine lady.

Nell Gwyn (1650–1687) is the most famous king's mistress in English history. It is reported that she was brought up in great poverty in Coal Yard Alley, near Drury Lane, that her father, a fruit seller, abandoned his family when she was very young, and that her drunken mother ran a brothel. Pretty, quick-witted Nell was a gifted comic actress. Her relationship with Charles II began in 1668, and the king fathered her two sons. Many anecdotes are told about her, including one that shows her popularity: when Nell was travelling through Oxford, her coach was mistakenly taken to be that of her French rival for Charles' favours, Louise de Kerouaille. A mob started to shout insults, so Nell put her head out of the coach window and shouted "Good people, you are mistaken – I'm the Protestant whore!" Nell Gwyn was buried in the Church of St Martin-in-the-Fields.

wurde sein Leichnam in einem mit Branntwein gefüllten Fass nach London transportiert und in St Paul's Cathedral in Anwesenheit von 32 Admirälen und mehr als 100 Seekapitänen in einem Marmorsarkophag beigesetzt. Er litt sein Leben lang an Seekrankheit.

Eliza Doolittle Covent Garden ist immer noch ein Theaterviertel. Die Idee für das Bühnenstück ‹Pygmalion›, das später zum Musical ‹My Fair Lady› umgearbeitet wurde, hatte George Bernard Shaw erst 1897, zwei Jahre nach den in diesem Buch beschriebenen Ereignissen. Als Sherlock Holmes sie aufsucht, ahnt Eliza Doolittle noch nicht, dass sie eines Tages als Schülerin des Phonetikprofessors Henry Higgins ihren Londoner «Cockney»-Dialekt ablegen und lernen wird, wie eine englische Dame zu sprechen.

Nell Gwyn (1650–1687) ist die berühmteste königliche Mätresse der englischen Geschichte. Es ist übermittelt, dass sie als Kind in ärmsten Verhältnissen in der Coal Yard Alley, nahe Drury Lane, lebte. Ihr Vater, ein Obstverkäufer, verließ die Familie früh, ihre trunksüchtige Mutter führte ein Bordell. Die hübsche und schlagfertige Nell war eine begabte Komödiantin. 1668 fing ihre Liaison mit Charles II. an, der mit ihr zwei Söhne zeugte ... Viele Anekdoten belegen ihre Beliebtheit. Als einmal Nells Kutsche durch Oxford fuhr, wurde sie mit der Kutsche der Rivalin in Charles' Gunst, der Französin Louise de Kerouaille, verwechselt. Auf die Beschimpfungen der Menge hin steckte Nell ihren Kopf aus dem Fenster und rief: «Ihr irrt euch – ich bin die protestantische Hure!» Nell Gwyn wurde in der Kirche St Martin-in-the-Fields beerdigt.

César Ritz (1850–1918) was a pioneer of the luxury hotel trade. In 1878 he became manager of the Grand Hôtel National in Lucerne, and held this position until 1888 while also running the Grand Hôtel in Monaco. In the following year he took over management of the newly built Savoy Hotel in London, but was dismissed along with chef Auguste Escoffier in 1897 after accusations of embezzlement: large quantities of fine wines and spirits had gone missing from the hotel cellars. Ritz and Escoffier then founded their own company and opened the Ritz Hotel in Paris.

Oscar Wilde (1854–1900) The Savoy Hotel was one of the main locations for the love affair between Oscar Wilde and Lord Alfred Douglas, which led to Wilde's imprisonment and indirectly to his early death. He was convicted of gross indecency on 25 May 1895, five weeks before Holmes and Watson visited the hotel.

William Shakespeare (1564–1616) was a playwright, actor and theatre manager. The written record reveals little hard evidence about his life, and the detailed biographies of Shakespeare have been constructed by means of inference and circumstantial information. He probably lived mainly in London from about 1587 until about 1613 and spent his last years in his home town, Stratford-upon-Avon, where he was buried in Holy Trinity Church.

William Marshal, 1st Earl of Pembroke (1146–1219), was a younger son of a noble family. Loyal service under four kings and his fighting prowess as, according to a chroni-

César Ritz (1850–1918) war ein Pionier des Luxushotel-
gewerbes. 1878 wurde er Leiter des Grand Hôtel National in Luzern und war bis 1888 gleichzeitig Manager des Grand Hôtel in Monaco. Im Jahr darauf führte
er das neu erbaute Savoy Hotel in London, wurde
aber 1897 gemeinsam mit seinem Chefkoch Escoffier
wegen Untreuevorwürfen entlassen: Große Mengen
teurer Weine und Spirituosen waren aus den Kellern
verschwunden. Daraufhin gründeten Ritz und Couf-
fier eine eigene Firma und eröffneten das Hotel Ritz in
Paris.

Oscar Wilde (1854–1900) Das Savoy Hotel war eine der
wichtigsten Kulissen der Liebesbeziehung zwischen Oscar
Wilde und Lord Alfred Douglas, die zu einer Gefängnisstrafe für Wilde und indirekt zu seinem frühen Tod führte.
Er wurde am 25. Mai 1895, fünf Wochen vor Holmes' Besuch im Hotel, wegen unsittlichen Verhaltens verurteilt.

William Shakespeare (1564–1616) war Bühnenautor, Schau-
spieler und Theatermanager. Es gibt wenige gesicherte
Kenntnisse über sein Leben, die detaillierten Biografien
über Shakespeare beruhen auf Mutmaßungen und Indizien.
Wahrscheinlich lebte er von ca. 1587 bis ca. 1613 vorwie-
gend in London und verbrachte seine letzten Jahre in seiner
Heimatstadt Stratford-upon-Avon, wo er in der Holy Trinity
Church beigesetzt wurde.

William Marshal, 1. Graf von Pembroke (1146–1219), war ein
jüngerer Sohn aus dem Adel. Treuer Dienst unter vier Königen und seine Tapferkeit als «größter Ritter, der je lebte»

cler, "the greatest knight who ever lived" made him the most powerful man in England at the end of his life, when he became regent in the minority of Henry III.

Sir Arthur Conan Doyle (1859–1930) was born in Edinburgh and studied medicine there. He began to write short stories while a student and in 1887 published his first novel, *A Study in Scarlet*, in which Sherlock Holmes made his first appearance. Conan Doyle's medical practice was not a success, but he quickly became famous and wealthy as an author, publishing four novels and 56 short stories featuring Sherlock Holmes over a 40-year period. However, he came to regard Holmes as a distraction from "higher" literature. By this he meant his historical novels, which have now largely been forgotten.

Conan Doyle campaigned against miscarriages of justice and exploitation in the Congo Free State. He was a keen footballer, golfer and cricketer, playing occasionally for Marylebone Cricket Club, and was one of the pioneers of downhill skiing in Switzerland. Patriotic motives led him to defend the British position in the Boer Wars, and he believed he owed his knighthood in 1902 to this.

The deaths of his first wife and elder son awakened an interest in spiritualism, and he was a member of the Ghost Club, which carries out scientific investigations into supernatural phenomena.

Sir Christopher Wren (1632–1723) earned a reputation for his scientific research in fields including astronomy,

(so ein Chronist) ließen ihn schließlich zum mächtigsten Mann Englands aufsteigen, als er Reichsverweser für den minderjährigen Henry III. wurde.

Sir Arthur Conan Doyle (1859–1930) wurde in Edinburgh geboren und begann während seines Medizinstudiums dort Kurzgeschichten zu schreiben. Seinen ersten Roman, ‹Eine Studie in Scharlachrot›, in dem Sherlock Holmes erstmals die Bühne betrat, veröffentlichte er 1887. Conan Doyles Augenarztpraxis war ein Misserfolg, aber als Schriftsteller wurde er sehr bald so erfolgreich, dass er in seiner über 40 Jahre langen Karriere insgesamt vier Romane und 56 Kurzgeschichten über Sherlock Holmes schrieb. Conan Doyle betrachtete Holmes als Ablenkung von «höheren Dingen», womit er seine heute vergessenen historischen Romane meinte.

Conan Doyle setzte sich für Opfer von Fehlurteilen und gegen Unrecht im Freistaat Kongo ein. Er war ein leidenschaftlicher Fußballer, Golfer, spielte gelegentlich für den Marylebone Cricket Club und gehörte zu den Pionieren des Skisports in der Schweiz. Als Patriot schrieb er ein Buch zur Verteidigung der britischen Position im südafrikanischen Burenkrieg und glaubte, dass er deswegen 1902 geadelt wurde.

Unter dem Eindruck des Todes seiner ersten Frau und seines älteren Sohns wandte er sich dem Spiritismus zu und wurde Mitglied im Ghost Club, der übernatürliche Phänomene wissenschaftlich untersucht.

Sir Christopher Wren (1632–1723), ein angesehener Forscher auf den Gebieten der Astronomie, Mathe-

mathematics and physics. He was a founder and later president of the Royal Society. His first forays into architecture date from his time as professor at Oxford University after 1663. In 1669 he was appointed King's Surveyor of Works and carried out many royal commissions. His architectural legacy can be seen at Hampton Court and Kensington Palace, and in Greenwich and Chelsea, as well as in churches in the City of London.

Sir Horace Jones (1819–1887) became architect and surveyor to the City of London in 1864. He was responsible for building Smithfield, Billingsgate and Leadenhall markets, and the Temple Bar monument at the west end of Fleet Street. He designed Tower Bridge but died soon after construction work started. His partner Sir John Wolfe-Barry, who then took charge of the project, was responsible for the Gothic adornments and for cladding the towers in stone instead of the brick facing that Jones had intended.

matik und Physik, war Gründer und später Präsident
der Royal Society. Erste Bauwerke stammen aus seiner
Zeit als Professor an der Universität Oxford ab 1663.
1669 wurde er zum königlicher Generalarchitekten er-
nannt und realisierte viele Auftragswerke. Zu seinem
architektonischen Vermächtnis gehören Residenzen wie
Hampton Court und Kensington Palace, Gebäude in
Greenwich und Chelsea sowie Londoner Kirchen.

Sir Horace Jones (1819–1887) war ab 1864 Stadtbau-
meister der City of London und für den Bau der Märkte
Smithfield, Billingsgate und Leadenhall sowie des
Temple-Bar-Denkmals am westlichen Ende der Fleet
Street zuständig. Er plante die Tower Bridge, verstarb
aber kurz nach Beginn der Bauarbeiten. Sein Partner
Sir John Wolfe-Barry führte das Projekt weiter und war
für die gotischen Verzierungen und die Verkleidung
der Türme in Naturstein statt Ziegelstein verantwort-
lich.

Inhalt

1. Sherlock Holmes' New Case · Ein neuer Fall für Sherlock Holmes
   221B Baker Street   8 · 9
2. A Meeting with the Prince Consort · Eine Einführung mit dem Prinzgemahl
   Buckingham Palace   22 · 23
3. Coronations and Tombs · Krönungen und Gräber
   Westminster Abbey   38 · 39
4. Gunpowder, Treason and Fists · Schießpulver, Hochverrat und Fausthiebe
   Houses of Parliament   60 · 61
5. A Famous Front Door · Eine berühmte Haustür
   Downing Street Nr. 10   74 · 75
6. The King and his Painter · Der König und der Malerfürst
   Banqueting House   90 · 91
7. A National Hero · Ein Volksheld
   Trafalgar Square   106 · 107
8. Roses and Oranges · Rosen und Apfelsinen
   Covent Garden   118 · 119
9. Celebrities and Scandal · Prominenz und Skandal
   Savoy Hotel   134 · 135
10. A Poet and a Knight · Ein Dichter und ein Ritter
    The Temple   150 · 151
11. A Literary Pub · Eine Literatenkneipe
    Ye Olde Cheshire Cheese   172 · 173
12. The Architect and his Dome · Der Architekt und seine Kuppel
    St Paul's Cathedral   186 · 187
13. A Marvel of Technology · Ein technisches Wunder
    Tower Bridge   204 · 205

The Detectives and their Witnesses · Die Ermittler und ihre Zeugen   222 · 223